Reflections Of A Town Driver
The Road To Redemption

©2025 Castlebrook LLC
All rights reserved. Published in 2025
Printed in the United States of America
First Edition

Paperback ISBN 979-8-218-83424-1
Hardcover ISBN 9798266283275
Library of Congress Control Number:
2022900895
Printed in the United States of America

This is the true story of one man's journey through the U.S. criminal justice system—a system that promised justice but does not always deliver on its promise. Every detail in these pages is grounded in fact. Names have been changed to protect privacy, but the events, the dates, and the voices you'll encounter are real. What follows is not just a personal account—it's a window into a broken system. Prepare to see it as you've never seen it before.

Praise for Reflections Of A Town Driver

What you are about to read is a unique story of a very successful businessman who was accused of a white-collar crime. He was sent to federal prison. As you read, you will learn that Chris becomes a driver for the prison at Fort Dix, NJ. He takes advantage of his driving job to gather insights about his inmate passengers' crimes, which are the subject of stories you will soon read. This book is compelling, emotional, and hard to put down. I refused to let go until I read the last word.
      Barbara Mazzarella, a long-time friend.

As a friend of the author, I had the unique privilege of reading this book as it was being written. On the surface, it offers a rare and unfiltered look into prison life, the choices that lead men there, and the far-reaching impact on their families. That alone makes it worth reading.
      But this book goes deeper. Its honesty is both refreshing and unsettling, pushing readers to contemplate loyalty, criminality, and empathy—without the discourse ever feeling preachy or forced. The vivid descriptions may shock some, and at times, the realities shared may seem unbelievable; however, they are true and accurate accounts.

I fully expect this book to earn at least four stars—and I believe you'll agree. It's a powerful, unforgettable read.

Foreword

Over the past years, I have often had flashbacks to my time at the prison Camp in Fort Dix, New Jersey. I have watched movies about guys in prison and wondered how stupid they could be to get into trouble. One day, I woke up on a cot surrounded by 400 men in the Federal Prison Camp and wondered how this had happened. You read stories about how people get into trouble, never imagining that it could be you. I spent five and a half years pondering what went wrong, and still can't figure it out.
This book is about my life, something I'm very proud of. A story of hope,
love, and redemption. How do you get back on your feet after a hard
fall? You have to move forward, or you lose.
    I worked as a driver for a US prison, transporting inmates who were being released and going home after years of incarceration. I was fortunate to meet men who had served their time. Some have become friends, while others will never be seen again. While back at the Camp, I jotted down the stories that were shared with me on the way to their freedom.

Time crawls when you are incarcerated. You think about family and what you're missing. Writing down the experiences that were shared with me became a great way to deal with my circumstances and pass the time.

This book started as a conversation with friends and has become an important part of my life. Sharing what happened to my family and what we went through feels like therapy; it eases the pain carried inside. I want to express my sincere gratitude to the friends who supported me in writing and publishing this book. Each one holds a special place in my heart. If this is successful, it's thanks to their hard work and insights.

Naeema Samira, thank you for all the time and effort you invested in getting this book to a stage worthy of consideration for publication. I could not have done this without you. All our conversations and the time spent made me push harder. I'm not a good listener, but I listened to you, and you were right.

CR Montoya, what a wonderful writer you are. I knew that after wanting to tell you about this book for years, you would be so helpful in bringing the people in this book to life. What a talent you are. Thank you for all the support and help.

Judy Turek, thank you. With a gift like yours, you look at a page full of words and make one suggestion that improves the entire book. When I sent the manuscript to you, I was nervous and afraid you would dislike it. When I opened my email and saw you loved it, I jumped out of my chair. Judy was the finishing touch to this special book. Judy is the closer when you need a win last inning with two outs. Judy is the person you reach out to.

Without my family's support, I might not have been able to write this book. I'm sure I wouldn't have come through this nightmare as the person I am today. They meant everything to me. My motivation to hold on to hope was knowing that better days lay ahead and that there would be a way to regain some sense of normalcy. Visits from my wife were something I cherished. Seeing Annie and searching her face for love gave me confidence that many inmates didn't have. Because of Annie and our children's constancy, I understood I would have time with them and our grandchildren. This made the unbearable more bearable.

In this topsy-turvy world of ours, few things are as meaningful or important as love. I have experienced it and continue to have it in abundance. I cannot find the words to express how much my wife, family, and the support of my friends have meant to me. They were the glue that kept me going and gave me the strength and will to write this book. While thank you seems trite, I thank them for helping me through this unexpected experience.

Preface

**"It is better to let the crime of a guilty person go unpunished than to condemn the innocent."
As stated in a 1895 US Supreme Court case.**

I can admit a lot of things now. I got lost, and that's the truth. Money and people changed and poisoned me. When I'd had enough, my thoughts kept saying more. Greed had changed me so much that the man in the mirror was unrecognizable.

The work I loved turned into something I began to hate. People and friends were drawn to me because of my money. I frowned at others to avoid looking at myself and to prevent auditing my actions. Now those dark clouds have lifted.

I am a privileged man. I don't say that to boast, but I'm not ashamed of it. Nothing was handed to me. My life started with humble roots. Success came through hard work and sacrifice; good luck contributed as well. This is my reality, and I accept it as it is. Prison didn't change this; it gave me a chance to pause and realize it. It created a space for reflection.

Most people are fortunate never to experience the Department of Justice's (DOJ's) inner workings. I have, and what follows are my thoughts on those experiences and situations that impacted my family and me. My observations are intended to inform readers about the system and how lives are changed by the circumstances an inmate must navigate. The Bureau of Prisons (BOP) is necessary because humans are fallible. We make mistakes. Some are heinous, while others are forgivable and warrant a true corrections system where detainees can learn and position themselves to become productive members of society.

What you will read describes how the system entangled me and what I learned, experienced, and discovered. You may think, *this is a work of fiction.* It is not fiction; it is a reality that men and women who have crossed or are accused of crossing the line face, along with my views of the resulting consequences.

Although the 1895 Supreme Court case cited above has been quoted and restated over the years, it remains as steadfast today as it was in 1895. The realities of my entry into the system and my path toward completing my sentence follow.

As the title suggests, I was a Town Driver, a job in which an inmate in this position drives inmates to a bus station, railroad, airport, or halfway house to begin their reentry into society. Each vignette presents the actual dialogue between my passengers and me. Some conversations are hopeful, some are worrisome, and others aim to give insight into a process in great need of reform.

A note to my readers: as you may suspect, dialogue between inmates can be colorful and filled with expletives and rancor. It was my choice not to include vulgar language. It is sometimes referred to in a way that conveys the nature of the language used.

What follows accurately depicts my experiences. I hope you enjoy it and maybe even learn a little about the 'Correctional System.' I ask you to decide if its name, *correctional*, describes how it functions.

Chapter 1 – The Initiation	3
Benji	14
Chapter 2 – Life's Turns And Twists	22
Al And His Wish For The Pot of Gold	29
Chapter 3 – A Jury Of My Peers	36
Paradise Or Hell	42
Chapter 4 – The Trial Resumes	51
Banking On A Big Pay Day	59
Chapter 5 – Running From The Red	66
The Three Bears	72
Chapter 6 – Spinning A Tale	78
Even Cops Get Stung	84
Chapter 7 – How Would This End	89
The Fish Story	98
Chapter 8 – Painful Progress	103
Chapter 9 – A New Reality	114
Paradise Lost	118

Chapter 10 – Introductions	**122**
No Safe Place	**125**
Chapter 11 – It's Never Enough	**131**
You Can't Always Go Back	**137**
Chapter 12 – Reaching For Some Control	**144**
Inspiration	**145**
Chapter 13 – Giving Back	**149**
They Called Him Biggs	**152**
Chapter 14 – A Helping Hand	**156**
The Last Dance	**163**
Chapter 15 – The Lights Are Back On	**169**
A Movie Plot - January 2020	**172**
Chapter 16 – Closing The Door	**178**
Afterword	**186**
Author's Note	**190**

Chapter 1 – The Initiation – June 2010

My attorney advised me that the trial would last two to three weeks. After this meeting, a dazed feeling from the enlightenment that had been shared. Stepping out on the street on a sunny day felt ironic. My mood had turned sour as I pondered the information that had just been delivered. Reaching for my phone, my home screen appeared. It was a photo of my wife, Annie, and me. She looks different now. In the photo, she was smiling. The day her smile disappeared was after my return home from a business trip. My job required me to travel back and forth to California, alternating weeks between the East and West Coasts.

This routine was initiated to reestablish relationships between our West Coast business partners and our East Coast executive teams. My JetBlue flight landed at JFK on a Friday at 6 am. Scurrying for a taxi, excited to be headed home. Annie was sitting on the couch in the den, waiting for my arrival. As was my routine when returning home, we hugged, enjoying each other's affection. I went upstairs, showered, and changed into something comfortable: gym shorts and a polo shirt. Annie had a hot cup of coffee waiting for me upon descending the stairs. We strolled to the kitchen, happy to enjoy breakfast together. Our daughter Shanna stopped by and joined in our feast of bagels. It was a nice, normal morning.

    My focus was on Annie as she moved around the kitchen. The early arrival of June heat was noticeable. Annie had started to tan. She looked as beautiful as on the day we met. Not that I would care, but she had managed to keep her figure after 22 years of marriage, countless Italian family dinners, and raising three kids. I felt like a lucky and grateful man.

    After breakfast, I went to my basement office and made work calls. While on a call, a knock at our front door caught my attention. Annie called for me to come upstairs. Her voice sounded strained and panicked. What was all the commotion about? I hastily ended my call and headed up. When I reached the living room, I was shaken by what I saw. There were six men, all wearing tactical vests. Four of them had handguns, and two carried large automatic weapons. It looked like a movie scene. Stunned and speechless, I stood there, trying to process what was happening. The blood drained from my face. Annie's usual healthy complexion had gone pale.

That day will never be forgotten. Confusion filled my thoughts. We lived in a nice, manicured neighborhood in Garden City, Long Island. I worked for a respectable company. What was happening? This wasn't a shakedown. This wasn't a robbery. This wasn't a targeted hit. This was the FBI looking for me.

They must have been at the wrong house. Someone had made an error, a major error. Why would a team of FBI agents be at my home? Without time to muster enough questions to wrap my head around the situation, I was handcuffed in the middle of my living room by one of the less-than-empathetic agents. My daughter and wife stared in disbelief. A sense of shock filled all of us, and a feeling of queasiness absorbed me. On June 10, 2010, I was arrested with no idea why. When questioning the agents, "Why are you arresting me?" I received no response. By persisting, and after the third request, the agent said, 'You violated the Travel Act.'"

That was all the agent said, leaving me wondering *what the hell the Travel Act is.*

Annie's smile had melted as the procession of FBI vehicles left our neighborhood with me, manacled, in the back seat of one of the black cars. It was a terrible, embarrassing moment. These events occurred more than three years ago, leading me to this *day in court*. One thing became clear: it's never simple dealing with this system. There were intermittent court dates for status meetings or hearings about the actual trial date. My lawyer advised me to waive my right to a speedy trial. I took his advice and stated my intent to the court, still confused about what was happening. After the preliminaries were over, the day arrived for jury selection.

Three years is a long time to wait for an event that you never wanted to come. We all lived through the uncertainty of pretending everything was okay when we understood it wasn't. Annie cried every day throughout the ordeal. At times, I pretended not to notice because she tried to hide her pain from me, but the look on her face and her swollen eyes suggested something different. Maybe that was selfish, trying to ignore what was coming and how it impacted her. The stress of what was whirling around us made me more self-absorbed. It was like trying to breathe underwater. With this shroud of darkness encircling us, Annie's puffy eyes were never void of love. Her heart was the same. Not being able to assure her that everything would be alright was suffocating. Her reactions were understandable; they had resulted from how troubled and worried she was. Being unable to comfort the love of my life or my family was like carrying our house on my shoulders.

When we entered the courthouse, the air in the foyer was stale and debilitating, portending what lay ahead. It was familiar, as it reminded me of the ride with the FBI on the day of my arrest. That day, New York traffic seemed to move slower than usual. Familiar streets looked foreign. Somewhere in Brooklyn, the FBI car entered an underground tunnel. I was taken inside a building, fingerprinted, and processed before being taken to the Federal Courthouse. Standing before a magistrate judge, he told me directly, "This is a serious crime, violating the Travel

Act." There were those words again: "The Travel Act."

There was no explanation, nothing to help me understand the accusations. Remembering that one of the FBI agents had said was the reason for my arrest did not help to lift the fog.

My lawyer explained that the Travel Act is like a blanket that covers several crimes. After looking it up, I learned that it's a federal crime to use the US Mail or engage in interstate or international travel to further certain *unlawful activities.* The Travel Act was intended to give federal law enforcement a way to fight organized crime. Thinking I've been arrested under the blanket of the Travel Act, is it because of my name, Christopher Finazzo? It seemed my arrest might be related to it. I worked my whole life not to be involved in any organized crime, now I'm a retailer charged with *mafia crime*? President John F Kennedy put this law into effect in 1961 to give the federal government the means to combat organized crime, when his brother Bobby was the Attorney General. I started to wonder what was going on; *what did the government think they had caught a retail crime boss?*

This act was the reason for my dilemma. I pleaded not guilty and was released on a $3 million bail. The extent of just how much of a mess I was in began to sink in. My thoughts raced like a bad movie on replay, fearing the possible outcomes.

It was now April 2013, and we were back in Brooklyn at the courthouse. Annie stood speechless by my side as we waited to enter. My case had been assigned to the U.S. District Court for the Eastern District of New York. As the clock ticked away our time, Annie's hand rubbing my back was my only comfort. Her touch was gentle. I blamed myself for drawing strength from her. Annie was fragile now, confused and troubled by what was happening. Her face wore a weariness that was unfamiliar to me. A dark cloud hung over us in the months and years after my initial appearance and posting bail. It was unrelenting, a constant intrusion into our lives. The conversations with lawyers seemed endless. My assets had been frozen. My family was hurting. Although I didn't understand why this happened, I blamed myself for our family's circumstances. I stared at the courtroom doors, anticipating when they would open, wondering what fate awaited me. I couldn't stand straight, feeling unworthy of my name and the reputation that was earned by my hard work. My pride was slipping away.

Our adult children were dazed into silence. They had many questions over the past three years, but none today. Shanna and her husband, Anthony, cared for my three-year-old granddaughter, Valentina. She was a bright light. I was grateful she didn't understand any of this. Hearing her giggle from a few rows behind me was comforting, knowing that she was untouched by what was unfolding. My son, Christopher, was occupied on his phone. He was successful in his own right. What was he thinking? Had my situation caused problems for him? I was most worried about Tony, my youngest son. He was sensitive like me, causing me concern about the impact this might have on him. Because we worked in the same industry, whispers about me circulated.

Had I disappointed him? Were they all disappointed? My personal sense of disappointment felt like a dark cloud surrounding me. They had the right to feel this way, too.

I inhaled deeply when the doors to the courtroom opened, taking time to exhale to gather myself. Following my lawyer into the courtroom, my family trailing me as we approached our seats, a sense of eyes studying me felt like mosquito bites. I was always told to make eye contact during a job interview. In my mind, the potential jury members were my interview panel. I tried to make eye contact with each of them. This was a bad idea, sensing they were thinking they would rather be elsewhere. Now, I had an awareness of what *judgment* was like. My mind began to race as I reflected on everything that led me to this moment.

The befuddling charges against me included accusations of mail and wire fraud. *How was that possible?* Those charges could amount to fourteen felonies, each carrying a penalty of up to 20 years in federal prison. I hired a well-respected and experienced law firm and was content to let them do their job. I had grown to consider my primary lawyer, Bob, a friend, never doubting his dedication or competence. Alan was the second lawyer on my team. While he wasn't the lead, it was clear that he was following the case and was providing valuable assistance to Bob. Bob informed me that my co-defendant had accepted a plea deal and was sentenced to forty-two months in federal prison because he agreed to the DOJ's terms to secure some leniency. He had a good chance of returning home within two years. I asked Bob what a deal would look like for me. When he mentioned that I would have to forfeit my right to appeal in the future, I stopped listening. I was innocent; I had no doubts about it. All my efforts were for the benefit of my employer. I was determined not to give up my right to appeal. Bob's statement seemed unreasonable to me. Why surrender that right, a right guaranteed by the Constitution? Without much thought, I decided against a plea deal, never discussing this option or my decision with Annie. Maybe that was selfish, too, even arrogant, but I chose to take my chances and reserve my right to appeal if the jury ruled against me.

Amidst all the angst, trust in my judgment started to slip away. Jury pools are meant to be composed of a defendant's peers. The very word *peers* made me nervous. I was getting bad vibes from them, which made me question my decision. Should I have given the plea deal more consideration? Perhaps hiring a female attorney would have been a better choice? A black female attorney may have given me an advantage. Bob was dressed in what looked like a tailored, designer suit. I didn't own anything tailored. Designer clothes are not my style. The pool of potential jurors may have thought my clothing selection was intended to avoid looking prosperous. They may have concluded that I had gone to the thrift store to buy a secondhand suit as an act of diversion. I am not the type of person to show off. I'm not "that guy." The shoes I wore have been mine for 20 years. The silent *judgment* of the jury was chilling. The pit of my stomach was stirring up a small storm. The urge to go into the hall and vomit was hard to control. I wanted to turn my head to see my family, to hear Valentina's laugh. I longed to see the love in my wife's tear-filled eyes. I could not summon the strength to not turn to them. The veins in my neck had swollen, and my knees weakened, ready to buckle and cascade me to the floor, like a sack of oats. Sitting when instructed, my eyes closed, and my head lowered, worrying about what would come next.

...

Benji - March 2017

The pickup was scheduled for 9 am. I enjoyed being the town driver. Among the job choices, this was a plum. The job entailed transporting prisoners after their release. My duties included driving them to airports, bus stations, railroad stations, and halfway houses. I was their bridge to freedom. Once they exited my vehicle, they were no longer on prison grounds. Their first step, if they choose, was toward a changed life. The expressions on some of my passengers' faces were a picture of remorse for their crimes. Other faces were full of anger. It was as if they believed they were the wronged ones, not their victims. Most of the time, they were glad to escape that dark place. Sometimes, they were belligerent. Benji is the only person breaking free today. He's an older Black man. His destination is the Trenton Transit Station, about a forty-minute drive from Fort Dix, New Jersey.

As I waited for the Corrections Officer (CO), time seemed frozen. Being incarcerated, you always want time to fly. When my passenger and the CO appeared, the Officer carried an air of superiority. His chest was puffed out, and his demeanor was of someone who looked down on others. He escorted Benji to the car. Benji seemed in no rush, as if moving in reverse. Once they reached the van, Benji handed me a black garbage bag that contained his belongings. He sat without a sound in the front seat as I put his bag in the trunk. After we buckled up, we headed toward the front gate. Benji gazed out the window, lost in thought. I tried to make small talk with everyone; it made driving less routine.

"How much time did you serve?"

He responded in a weak voice, "Thirty-one years."

Benji grew up in Harlem. As a fellow New Yorker, we hit it off right away. He was soft-spoken and probably around seventy. Sometimes, guys come out looking great, as if time passed in days rather than years. The years had been hard on Benji. He looked defeated. His eyes were dull, lacking any sparkle. When you're in prison, all you see are the same drab walls, disconnected from the world inmates once knew. As I drove, Benji's gaze was fixed on the changing scenery. I recalled my first trip and how seeing the outside world was a joy beyond my expectations. Maybe Benji was feeling the same way.

Then, his head drooped and swayed; his voice cracked before he lost his composure and began to cry. This was not a new experience for me; these *tough guys* break down like anyone else. I reassured Benji that everything would be okay. He shook his head. He was a defeated man.

Benji was going home after spending thirty-one years in maximum—and low-security facilities nationwide. The thought of the word made him tremble. Prison had been his life, his home; he had nothing else.

"Listen, man, I have nothing to go home to. My parents and sister are dead. I *don't have no* family. I cried because this place was my life. I had friends who understood me. They understood what I've been through."

I can attest that being in prison isn't a good life, so it spoke volumes to me about how his prison experience had failed this man. Benji cried because he had to leave prison. He had to leave the meals, the game, and the guys he could relate to. Benji sighed and rolled down his window, welcoming the crisp air. There was still snow on the ground. I waited for Benji to calm himself before starting more conversation.

"Benji, what were you in for?"

"I committed a drug crime during a time when you got a long sentence for doing so. I was the fall guy for a big drug deal that went bad. I didn't do what the government said. I was a small piece of a much larger gang."

My impression was that Benji lacked the organizational skills, manpower, or funds to carry out the type of drug deal he was charged with. The men he worked for, the bosses, promised that if he took the fall, they would take care of his family as a gesture of their gratitude. Benji agreed, only to find out that his family would not be helped. His bosses betrayed him. Benji said he was part of an international drug ring with many moving parts. His role was to distribute drugs to the black community in Harlem. He was familiar with the neighborhood because he grew up on

114th Street, a close-knit, diverse area. During his youth, Benji said he was a good student and athlete. I asked him to explain, but he couldn't clarify why he got involved in the drug game. He couldn't even explain his actions to himself. Like many others with little, the lure of money was too strong to resist. As we approached the train station, Benji became less conversational. He sat staring, contemplating his next move.

Downtown Trenton is a downtrodden area. He seemed amazed by the number of people on the street and how dirty it looked.

"The station is only ten minutes away. Where are you going to stay?"

"No halfway house for me. Prison is my home. Those guys are my family. Now, I have nothing."

Benji stopped talking when the car stopped. I exited and retrieved Benji's bag from the trunk. It struck me that after being locked up for 31 years, all Benji had was one black garbage bag of belongings. I walked to the other side of the vehicle and opened Benji's door.

"Benji, it's time for you to leave. We're here."

Benji looked at me and started to cry again, this time sobbing. He told me he couldn't move his legs; they were frozen. I lied and said I had another pick-up, and he needed to get out.

"Listen, man, I can't move my legs. I don't *wanna*."

He insisted that he couldn't move his legs. For the next few minutes, I encouraged Benji, telling him he would be fine and that the shelter would take care of him and provide him with what he needed until he figured things out. Not sure if this was true, but I said it anyway. My responsibility was to get back to the Camp within the allotted time or face the consequences, which could include losing my job. Benji needed to get out. With my help, Benji finally got out of the car. He stood before me, searching my face for answers I did not have.

He looked up at me, "I want to go back."

It was hard to believe that life at Fort Dix was better than what awaited Benji, but I suspected it was true. Benji was left on the sidewalk in front of the Trenton Transit Station. He had $16.50 for a train ticket to reach New York Penn Station, $279 from his commissary account, instructions on how to find the shelter, and his black garbage bag. Looking in the rearview mirror, Benji hadn't moved. He stood in the same spot; his eyes closed, his head bowed. It was a sad sight, though this scene was becoming all too familiar.

Chapter 2 – Life's Turns And Twists – April 2013

We had been at court for hours. Nauseous, confused, and deflated best described my feelings sitting at the defendant's table. Glancing toward the jury pool was a mistake. Each look contributed to my confused feelings. A smile crossed my face when the clerk announced that the court would stand in recess. This would give me a chance to breathe some fresh air. Annie followed me out of this small jail. She pulled me aside and gave me a pep talk, hoping to calm my nerves. At that moment, it struck me how caring Annie was and her determination to be my comforter.

    Life can bring us challenges. This was one I could have never imagined. I was concerned about our children and our granddaughter. My hopes were for our boys to grow up in a house full of love, just like I did. My father was a welder, and my mother was a homemaker. We had a house at 1309 Crosby Avenue, Bronx, New York. We were lower middle class, but my parents ensured that my two sisters and I didn't feel like we missed out on anything. My maternal grandmother and my uncle moved in with us. My grandmother helped my mother around the house, cooking and cleaning. My uncle worked and contributed to paying the mortgage. My paternal grandparents lived in the house next to us. We were a big, happy, strong, religious family. This was my life's goal, and now, for reasons I still did not comprehend, my role would be missing.

All my working life, I buried myself in my job. I was a floor manager at Macy's department store, determined to succeed in my career. My hard work paid off as I was rewarded upon reaching or exceeding in my assigned duties.

A coworker surprised me when she said she wanted to introduce me to someone. I had no interest in dating and never alluded to wanting to meet anyone. I especially had no interest in meeting a stranger who could complicate my life. I had married too young, and as they say, it didn't stick. We had two sons, and involvement with a woman could add unwanted complications to an already busy life. Dating could grow into a serious commitment. I expressed my disinterest to my coworker Cathy, but she was intent on playing matchmaker.

It started with, "Chris, you're such a nice guy. You should get out there. You can't just work all the time. Let me introduce you to someone."

Cathy was well-intentioned and persistent. While walking the showroom floor one day, she said, "Chris, just hear me out. My husband works with a woman named Annie. He talks about her all the time and speaks highly of her. I think she might be the perfect woman for you!"

I didn't respond. I gave her a look that said, "This again?" It seemed clear she was not going to let it go.

"Come on, just meet her."

Cathy told me that Annie was an Assistant Bond Broker who lived in Queens and had a 6-year-old daughter. I had reservations, not because of anything Cathy said but because of myself. Still, to oblige, I took Annie's phone number.

I called Annie's number for a week. Each time, my greeting was a busy signal. In hindsight, it seemed I was ready to get back out there. Maybe Cathy was right; it was time.

Why else would I have called so many times? Not wanting to admit, I missed a woman's companionship, but I did. My work kept me busy, which helped me avoid facing this truth. Despite multiple attempts to reach Annie, a busy signal was my reward. I went from being interested to frustrated, feeling like a stalker and then a fool. After repeated failures, I gave up.

As expected, Cathy was upset about me abandoning her matchmaking mission. She made me promise to try calling Annie one more time. I didn't argue. That night, I was mainly motivated by the need to sleep. Still, after eating some takeout and finishing a beer, I called Annie's number again. This time, she answered.

We didn't talk for long. We exchanged pleasantries, and I asked her out on a date. Not wanting to waste this opportunity, we agreed to meet the following week, on Tuesday night, for dinner in Little Italy in Manhattan. The next day at work, Cathy was ecstatic with my update.

"I just know you will love her!"

Cathy was enthusiastic; my excitement surpassed hers.

Reflections Of A Town Driver

On the night of our date, it rained. I was glad she agreed to let me pick her up from home since I was running several hours late. I was off to a bad start, but I was working on a project that needed to be completed. Then, I got turned around trying to find her house. I didn't call so that she couldn't cancel. I had been looking forward to this dinner. Had we planned to meet her at the restaurant, she would have left after thirty minutes. Once I reached Annie's house, I breathed a sigh of relief. She answered her door, much to my surprise, smiling. She was not at all angry. She was comforting, reassuring me that my delay was not a problem. Grateful for her understanding, we headed to the city and the restaurant.

At dinner, we talked with ease as we ate our favorite selections from the menu: pasta for her and veal piccata for me. The restaurant was not crowded, which made for a more congenial setting. I was not thinking about work for the first time in a long time. During our meal, I grasped that my dinner companion was a beautiful woman. When I picked her up, the woman who opened the door was attractive. I didn't realize how striking she was in my panic about being late. What was equally impressive was her kindness. After dinner, a thought came to me, *This is the nicest woman I've ever met.*

    After a few dates with Annie, I was smitten. I attended her work events. Annie and I met for dinner often. There were times when we met just to talk. I took her to the ballet at Lincoln Center. I will never forget that date because Annie fell asleep before the ballet started, and it was a deep sleep! The gentleman on her other side allowed his shoulder to be her pillow. I let her sleep for an hour before I woke her to leave. Still, I was happy to be in her company. The heart is a funny creature; it seems to know real love. My heart didn't take long to help me understand that I wanted to spend the rest of my life with her.

    My relationship with Annie, which had become serious, introduced me to feelings that I had never experienced. We dated for five years before I asked her to marry me. Five years weren't needed to be sure that Annie was right for me. After a few dates, the thought that she was the one was constant in my heart and mind. Being unfamiliar with the ways of little girls, my desire to learn was strong. My connection with Annie's daughter, Shanna, grew like a flower blossoming in the morning sun. Like her mother, she was the epitome of sweetness. She would often accompany us on our dates, and it was wonderful. Shanna always greeted me with a big smile, which soon included the biggest hugs. Her father was not present in her life. Annie hinted that he was not a good guy, and I was content trusting her judgment and happily stepped into the father figure role in Shanna's life.

With two sons, I didn't want to overwhelm them with my developing relationship. We took our time introducing the kids. I thought they would like Annie, though unsure how they would handle seeing me with a woman who was not their mother. To my delight, they accepted Annie and Shanna's presence in our lives. Thinking back, it was a seamless process. The five of us became inseparable. My dates with Annie became family events. We attended sporting events, dinners, and vacations together with the kids. It became clear to both of us that our blended family would work.

All the kids were gathered on the day I proposed. They jumped around the house with the excitement of children on Christmas morning when I asked Annie to be my wife. She didn't hesitate to say *yes*. We married on January 13, 1990. Marrying her was the best decision of my life. She is the best thing that has ever happened to me.

...

Al And His Wish For The Pot of Gold - July 2016

As the town driver, I'm on call day and night. This day was mundane, but the night was unexpected. On rare occasions, a call comes in for an immediate release. That's when a court case is overturned or an appeal is won. In such instances, the inmate is notified that he will be released when the BOP is notified. Once the BOP has received this notice, it acts with urgency to avoid any liability should the inmate incur an accident. The inmate might not fully understand the reason for the release, but he's headed home.

I got called to the Officer's Station. "Be ready at 11:30 pm to take the immediate-release inmate to the Philly bus station." I had a little time to relax before 'the count.' Every night across the United States, at 9:30 pm sharp, federal prison facilities conduct a universal count. Each inmate must stand near his bunk. Then, we wait to be counted. Sometimes, the count is delayed because an inmate is in the shower, using the bathroom, or somewhere they shouldn't be. We stay in place until the count is finished. If the CO miscounts, which happens more than you might suspect, the process starts again. The count must match the number in the federal database for the facility. If the CO miscounts two or three times, they must do a bed bunk count. This requires that the inmates stand at our bunk bed, show their identification card, and say their name and inmate number aloud. The CO will then scratch our name off the roster. It may sound archaic, but that's how they ensure that no one has escaped.

    The count was cleared by 9:50 pm that night. All activities are suspended until the clear is announced. I prepared myself for the nighttime drive. I needed to pick up the inmate on the West Side of the complex. The complex consists of two low-security units and the Camp. There was no need to go to the garage because a 12-passenger van was left outside for evening use. I picked up the van keys and a flip phone programmed only to call the prison at the Officer's Station. Town Drivers must call when an inmate is dropped off or if the driver encounters an issue. You must be trusted to do this job, but that trust doesn't extend too far. Town Drivers are still inmates, and I was no different than the others.

At 11:30 pm, I was waiting in the van. A lieutenant escorted the inmate to the vehicle. As they approached, I thought he looked like someone I could befriend. He was an older gentleman, black, maybe around sixty years old. He was muscular, but just slightly—not a hulk like some of the other inmates.

The Lieutenant greeted me, "Finazzo, how are you?" Before I could answer, he continued, "If you have any trouble, call the Officer's Station at the Camp, and call when you're coming back."

The routine was etched into my memory. Nonetheless, I replied, "Yes, Sir."

Al got in the van's front passenger seat and started chatting. He was a talker.

Reflections Of A Town Driver

"I'm being released after serving 20 years. I got caught selling drugs on a military base. I had a nice landscaping business. I had good contracts, making decent money. I hooked up with some guys and started selling drugs on the base."

He served 20 years of a 25-year sentence. He had been called to his CO that afternoon and was stunned to hear that he was being released that day. His facial expression was between disbelief and a child who had just received a long-desired toy. A phone call with his son a few hours prior added to his amazement.

"I called my son and said, 'Son, I'm coming home. They're releasing me tonight. I'm taking a bus to Houston. It should take 23 hours. I can't believe it.'"

Calls in prison are timed and monitored. Inmates pay for them with whatever meager money they earn from their Camp job or money from family or friends. Most guys don't have much in their account, as the hourly pay rate for most jobs is just pennies. Al was grinning when he spoke about the call. I didn't know him, but the smile on his face made me happy for him.

He said, "Before prison, I lived in Houston. When I got locked up, I told my wife to divorce me. I couldn't ask her to wait for me. I wasn't going to be able to provide for her. I wanted her to go on with her life. I figured it would be easier on her and easier on me. I wrote her a few letters and sent an occasional card. Always wishing her well. The letters weren't enough, and we both stopped writing after a while. When I learned of my release, I asked my son to find me a place to live. I asked him to find a place near him in Dallas."

I asked Al if his son objected to his request. When you first get released from prison, you must return to the city of your last residence, in Al's case, Houston. It seemed logical that, without his wife, he would want to relocate to be near his son as soon as possible.

Al said, "He had other plans for me."

"Like what?" My curiosity had been piqued. When Al told me the plans, I fully understood the smile on his face.

"My son said, 'Dad, I can't find you a place near me. You're going home, Dad.'"

At first, I didn't follow what my boy was saying. Then he said, 'Mom never divorced you. She wants you home. She wants you to return to the life you guys built together. Dad, she never stopped loving you. She wants you to come home.'"

As Al relayed this part of his life to me, his expression changed as he became emotional and started to cry. This guy thought his world would be forever changed after serving a 20-year prison sentence. He imagined being released from prison and having no wife, no home, and no one to care for him.

He said, "I told my wife to move on with her life. I told her I was no good for her. That I had let her down. I said she should move on. I always assumed that she had, but she didn't! She's been waiting all this time for me. After all this time, she still loves me. She wants me home."

Al cried for the next thirty minutes. I understood his tears. Leaving prison is different for everyone; it's a major adjustment. In my estimation, only a few things can heal the wounds of a person's prison sentence— time, if there is enough of it, and love. Al was dropped off at the bus station to travel back to Texas and be reunited with his wife. I can say now that this trip was different from others. It seemed that a happy ending was almost certain.

Chapter 3 – A Jury Of My Peers – April 2013

The entire jury selection process was a mess. No one in the jury pool had ever heard of the Travel Act, an obscure law that few people understood. Attempts to explain it seemed as successful as trying to explain Einstein's Theory of Relativity to toddlers. The potential jurors included a truck driver, a small business owner, and a teacher. New Yorkers tend to have a no-nonsense attitude, and this group was no different. The selection process was stressful, but I sat through it, trying to hide my inner turmoil. Being in the courtroom was unavoidable for me. It was the last place any defendant wants to be. The room gave off *negative vibes* that I couldn't shake. I felt my eyes rolling and my lips pursing throughout the process. These automatic reactions now occurred at the slightest comment.

    Given the nature of the case, it was clear that my financial situation was stronger than that of the jurors. Did my appearance and life experience make me seem like a wealthy *white man* who didn't deserve their sympathy? They didn't know that I had worked hard for my success. Sure, I had help along the way, but I put in the effort. Still, nobody ever sees the struggle. After two days of multiple rounds of questions and answers, a diverse group of men and women was chosen to serve on the jury. The United States versus Christopher Finazzo was ready to move forward.

  The trial started in April 2013, the day after the jury selection. Seated next to my lawyer, I replayed all the events that led me to this point. Of all the things I questioned, the one thing that nagged me the most was my relationship with my former boss and supposed friend. Maybe I was paranoid; the stress made me feel like the earth was on my shoulders. Despite my best efforts, I'm certain the clinching of my jaws was evident to the jury whenever his name was mentioned. He was the CEO of the teen apparel retailer we had worked for. His version of the matter was, I was involved in a kickback scheme to line my pockets. On the company's organizational chart, I reported directly to him at the end of my tenure there, but my relationship with him had started well before my time at the clothing chain.

    When we first met, I was 30 years old and a buyer for young men's activewear at Macy's. He had come to the company from Bloomingdale's to be the Senior Vice President (SVP) of Menswear/Merchandise and President of the ready-to-wear division. He began working at Macy's a few years before I started and didn't hesitate to mentor me.

    This new SVP was unlike the guys I grew up with. As a child, all my friends lived on the same block. We would walk or ride our bikes together daily, and on hot summer days, we would swim in the small pool in my parents' backyard. Their siblings were like family, as mine were to them. Everyone looked out for each other. Our families left their front doors unlocked so we could wander from house to house at our leisure. There was an inherent trust that was built over time. It was the trust that the local butcher gave to my mother, allowing her to buy meat on credit by writing what she owed on a brown paper bag. It was a trust that comes from knowing someone beyond what you see on the surface. I didn't have that with this boss, at least not for a long while. Our relationship started because we were work colleagues. We didn't have much in common. He came from a wealthy family and had attended an Ivy League school. He was a handsome guy who oozed confidence. My modest upbringing, city college education, and empathic personality were in stark contrast.

Notwithstanding, my mentor was a straightforward guy, which I liked. He was also arrogant, which I didn't like. Arrogance aside, he could be very charming, so people, especially women, gravitated toward him. We had to attend many of the same work events, and his personality grew on me as we did. Over time, I started to think that he was okay. It became evident this was a miscalculation on my part.

I had worked for him at Macy's for five years when rumors about possible indiscretions with young women we worked with arose. The rumors could have been started by guys who were envious of him, or maybe the female staff gossiped about his flirtatious ways. The stories blossomed like a game of telephone. I didn't know and didn't care. This guy was married to a lovely woman.

I ignored the chatter about my work partner and his wife as they were becoming good friends. I wanted to believe he was a good person and that the noise grew out of jealousy due to his success. During that time, I married Annie, officially adopted Shanna, and settled into a caring family routine.

When the day of Shanna's wedding arrived, Annie looked like an angel. Justin attended the wedding with his wife. The wedding was a wonderful occasion. We all enjoyed the evening. We danced, laughed, and enjoyed the company of our friends and family.

Between my work and Annie's promotion to a bond broker, we purchased a home together after we were married. It had enough room for our blended family to be safe and comfortable. Before long, much to my delight, our house was like my childhood home. There were many laughs, loud dinners with extended family, and abundant love. My career was also moving in a great direction. My time at Macy's taught me a lot about the retail clothing industry, which inspired me to try establishing my clothing brand.

Determined to make my mark on the fashion world, I approached my boss with the news. As was his style, he had a few questions. I shared my idea with him about an athletic brand, leveraging my expertise in trends for young adult men, which sparked a strong desire to explore this area. Unlike the other managers, he was supportive and helpful with my transition.

I tendered my resignation in late 1992 to start my clothing line. I called my brand *In The Paint*, referencing the painted area on the basketball floor for players to score high-percentage shots. I leveraged all my contacts to get the project off the ground. With a team of six staff members and subcontractors as needed, In The Paint was born. I hired designers, coordinated production using domestic and foreign manufacturers, and secured marketing professionals. The company grew at a rapid pace, and I was ecstatic. Justin was impressed with my brand and helped to place some of my products at Macy's. I was grateful for his assistance. Eventually, I secured an NBA licensing deal, which led to my brand being carried in Foot

Locker stores, first regionally and then across the country. Life was good!

When the time and market were right, I sold *my baby*. In my mind, I had officially *made it*. But the desire for having more was still strong. Annie and the kids were happy, but why was this not enough? I had everything I should have wanted, having tasted success, and now I wanted a bigger bite.

Now, seated in a courtroom, seeing my former boss and colleague, a person I once called a friend, on the witness stand made me realize that I was not driven by mere career aspirations but by greed and envy. Listening to this *stranger's* testimony, I thought *I must be losing my hearing; he couldn't have said those things.* Anger grew within me towards him and myself.

...

Paradise Or Hell - March 2018

It's a foggy day in Fort Dix, New Jersey. We are off to a late start. Procedures demand that we have a fog count. Before arriving here, I didn't know what that was, but it's a primitive way of tracking inmates to ensure no one disappeared by some magic away in the fog. When I think about it, I recall an old 1930s movie where the prisoners desperately run through thick, hazy clouds, hoping for an unhindered escape. If you are incarcerated in the northeast of the United States at a government prison facility, you will experience a fog count.

The fog cleared at 8:30 am, so my day could start. Next stop the garage to pick up my van and then my passenger. Only one person, Tito, needed transport.

Tito was headed to Puerto Rico. As he got in the car, he asked me how long it would take us to reach the airport. I told him it should take one hour with traffic. Tito looked the part of a guy going to the electric chair. He was a bundle of nerves as he sat in the front passenger seat of the minivan.

He wasn't carrying anything. He was going to a halfway house for six months to acclimate back into society. He asked me what he should do once we reached the airport. I explained everything, including the security checkpoint, check-in procedure, and boarding. I asked Tito what he did to land himself in prison.

He said, "I was running guns through a funeral parlor. Imagine that we used a funeral procession to run guns."

His statement was delivered in his best version of street talk. My ears burned listening to him. When he noticed my surprised expression, a small smirk spread across his face. Tito seemed to sense that I wanted to know more. It appears people like Tito survive by reading others. I needed to work on my poker face.

I turned to look at him and said, "You have my attention; tell me what happened."

"I was hired at a funeral home in Ponce, Puerto Rico, to work with the traffic department. My job was to stop the traffic at the traffic lights using my car so the funeral procession could go through. I had done this several hundred times and was familiar with how things worked on the streets in Ponce. One day, a group of guys approached me. They wanted to move guns from the Caribbean to Puerto Rico. They wanted to use the funeral procession to hide what they were doing. They said that by placing the guns in a casket, they could freely move them through the streets without suspicion. They figured, 'Who would suspect that guns would be traveling in a casket?' It was too sick for anyone to catch on.'"

My first thought was *wow, this is a tall tale*, but the more he spoke, the more details indicated it was true. Tito said he worked only a few days a week at the funeral parlor and earned little money.

He continued, "Ponce was full of crime and drugs, and guns were a big part of the culture. The people who approached me offered me lots of f..ing money. More money than I had ever seen."

He explained that most of the time, the local police would provide an escort through the streets for funerals.

"The plan sounded perfect, man. *Ya* know. Big bucks for easy, no-sweat work."

This side gig allowed him to make extra money to help his family. Tito agreed to help move the guns, did his part, and never encountered any problems.

Then, the situation changed: "One day, a new driver showed up to work at the funeral parlor. He was a young guy who claimed to be from San Juan, the northern part of the island. I was told he was added to the staff as a favor to the owner's cousin. The new guy, Jose, seemed to know a lot about the funeral business. Jose said he moved to Ponce to gain more experience. He said his friends had agreed to invest in a funeral home in a smaller city, and he would be *The man*."

Tito said he had been working with Jose for about two months when, one day, Jose asked, "Man, how do you survive on this lousy salary?"

Tito said he never mentioned his side work but suspected Jose was seeking evidence about the illegal enterprise.

Tito continued, saying, "There was a big funeral on the schedule. A popular older man in town had passed away. Lots of the town's people were expected to show up for the burial. It was going to be a busy day. That morning, I placed guns in the casket and then secured the corpse."

I didn't ask Tito how many guns he stashed, but I wished I had.

He continued, "A police escort led the procession, and the police also directed traffic. I was told to drive the family in a car behind the hearse. I had done this before, so it didn't seem odd."

We were close to the airport with ten minutes left in our trip. I hoped our ride didn't end before Tito's story.

"At one of the intersections, the police stopped the hearse, and all the cars in the line stopped. Unmarked cars pulled up from every direction. The federal police got out of their cars, wearing full assault gear. They were holding high-powered guns. Everyone exited their vehicle. I swallowed hard. They were there for me. I dropped to the ground, 'ATF, FBI, get on the ground was repeated as if on replay!' Trouble had caught up with me.

"They had warrants to open the casket. I couldn't see who said it, but an agent said, 'We got *em*. They're in the casket.' The ATF collected all the hidden guns."'

Tito said that he later learned that on the morning of that day's procession, the ATF and FBI raided the homes where the leaders of the gun smuggling operation lived. A local police officer advised Tito to disclose all information about the movement of illegal arms, explaining that cooperation would make things easier for him and his family.

Tito added, "I remember when the line of cars came to a halt. Jose was nowhere to be seen. He had been driving behind me when we left the funeral parlor. When the police surrounded us, it felt as if he had vanished. I never saw him again, assuming he was working as an undercover agent for the ATF. I found out that the men who initially approached me were under investigation for a long time. Someone talked, and it wasn't good for everyone. Forty-nine of us went down."

Tito said that despite being asked repeatedly by ATF agents, he didn't know where the guns came from or how long they had been moving into Puerto Rico. Tito served a sentence of forty-six months between Puerto Rico's Metropolitan Detention Center in Guaynabo and Fort Dix.

Tito told me he would "keep it legal" from now on. I wished him well with his second chance.

Chapter 4 – The Trial Resumes – April 2013

My former boss, the witness, occasionally glanced my way as he spoke under oath. It was difficult to look at him; it was like watching a stranger. In his own words, he described the ebb and flow of our communication over the years. His selective memory glossed over many details that would reveal my true character, as they might cast him in a negative light. He had been questioned by the FBI and needed to be consistent with what he told them. He must have minimized our friendship because his comments did not reflect our relationship. He wanted to project the sense that we were not close. We were just work colleagues, not much more. He wanted the lights to shine on me and no one else.

Macy's, in 1987, started a brand called Aéropostale. At the time, the company began marketing this product line in response to a similar offering from the GAP. This was their attempt to establish a specialty store. The team that reported to Justin was instrumental in building the Aéropostale brand. The new brand was growing. Justin sought a new opportunity and left the company to pursue it.

The brand was losing a lot of money, and Justin was hired as its president. His primary task was to get the brand on track and make it profitable. It was a big task, and the new president's plate was already full. Stress from the job had taken a toll on his marriage. This, coupled with raising the four kids he and his wife shared, led to his loss of focus and increased demands on the entire team. He was a man drowning on land when I received his call.

While his behavior left me with a bad taste, I still regarded him as a friend. We spoke weekly on the phone but did not socialize outside of work. I remember that one particular call was work-related, just as suspected.

He said, "I have no idea what the f... I'm doing here; I need your help. Come and speak to me."

I made plans to meet him to learn more about his new position with Macy's. When we met, he explained that the Aéropostale brand was not doing well. The products and marketing were not what the teen customers wanted. To make matters worse, Macy's had opened Aéropostale stores nationwide without a plan. By Justin's admission, he was not a good merchant and had no clear vision.

"This is where you can help, Chris."

Merchandising was a first love, and I was good at it. With a background in retail dating back to my teenage years, and my recent success with *In the Paint,* made me an ideal choice to assist. When Justin asked for my help, he didn't sugarcoat the label's dire situation; it was in trouble. They had just lost $13 million in sales revenue. If I could help him turn it around, it would be the next significant step in my career.

"You are the best merchant I know."

It was a lot to think about; my wife and three children were my priority. It was imperative for me to make the right decision to ensure my family's well-being. Working for a struggling company was risky, but the potential reward could be substantial.

I agreed to return to Macy's and help with the challenge. Annie was supportive of my decision. Our home life was fantastic; my eagerness to get back to work was evident in my restlessness. Annie had sensed my pent-up energy. In July 1996, I was hired as the Merchandiser for Men's Wear for the new chain. It didn't take long to realize that what had been shared with me was correct. The brand's status was poor. The structure was chaotic. There was no organization; the product didn't meet the customers' wanted, and the store teams wanted the "old Aéropostale" back. To make matters worse, the team was unfocused and struggled to understand how to adjust the merchandise. Many key players were leaving to join other retailers.

    I was running the men's side of the house, but women's also had problems. The industry models indicated that, based on current trends, our women's merchandise should have reflected seventy percent of our sales, but it only reflected thirty. We needed to adjust to grow the brand. Private-label brands like Abercrombie & Fitch, American Eagle, and many others had a stronghold on the teen market. They were the varsity players, and we were the junior hopefuls. Our collections needed updates to reflect the times. This was clear to me, though our leadership was freewheeling and not focused on what needed to change. Our teams were divided into merchants, planners, allocation design, and production; it was evident that the design team was running the show. The problem was they were not designing things that our customers wanted.

The pressure was mounting to change our business practices and offer more sought-after products. The issues were obvious to me. I needed full authority to make the changes. While attempting to make compelling arguments for a new direction, my efforts often met with resistance. It was very frustrating. The goal was to find ways to improve the situation, which required me to be given the support to do so.

My days were filled with an abundance of caffeine and stress. I was not alone; the entire team, from top to bottom, was in the same position. During this time, my relationship with Justin began to develop outside of work, which occurred as a natural consequence of the time we were spending together. We worked long hours and traveled with other team members for overseas meetings, forming a genuine bond that eventually extended beyond the workplace through late-night drinks, early-morning meetings, and long flights. As our relationship grew, it started to feel like my authentic childhood friendships. I found myself wanting to be in his inner circle—a circle that, learned, did not suit me well, making me feel ashamed of my actions.

    We were on a flight home to New York from Hong Kong the day before Thanksgiving 1997. I was looking forward to seeing Annie and the kids; the flavors of the variety of food and desserts that would blanket our dinner table were already bubbling in my head. The thought of this, combined with our successful meeting in Hong Kong, put me in a great mood. I saw the results of my hard work over the previous year start to pay off, feeling thankful for the progress.

    Justin, on the other hand, seemed agitated. During the flight, I asked him if he was okay. He brushed me off at first, but I had gotten to know him well enough to realize that something was bothering him, like trouble at home. The stress had impacted his home life, and he and his wife were still struggling. I wanted the best for him and his family, and not a breakup. He had four children, who needed both parents. Although I rebounded after my first marriage, it wasn't clear to me that Justin would be so fortunate, given his struggles from all the pressure at work. My thought was to help in any way possible. Pressing him to share what was on his mind, what he said shocked me. It was not his marriage that was worrying him. He told me that Macy's was going to sell Aéropostale.

 I wanted to think this was some sick joke, but the look on Justin's face made it clear he was serious. He was still processing the news himself and looked unhappy about it. Now, his agitation was understandable. We were on the flight to New York with a dedicated team of colleagues who were at risk of losing their jobs. He didn't dare share this news with everyone the day before Thanksgiving. When I pressed for details, my questions were met with a stone face and no specifics. How could he tell me that and expect me to sit quietly? It was the day before Thanksgiving, for God's sake. Christmas was around the corner. I was in disbelief. My feelings were mixed—wanting to collapse and scream. I had never experienced this before; one thought was to punch something, and my tormentor would have been a suitable target.

When the plane landed, I fixed my eyes on my fellow traveler. He was a friend, and my worries extended to him, myself, and our entire team. I needed to talk to him more, and I was certain he could provide additional information. We gathered our belongings from the overhead compartment and started deplaning. As we cleared customs, my chance to speak with him privately arose. I pulled him aside, but his agitation did not fade.

"You can't just drop a bomb like that."

"What do you want me to say, Chris?" he asked. "Their minds are made up. They are going to sell."

His tone was cold. I'll never forget what he said when asked,

"What does that mean for us?"

"They are going to make me the President of the Furniture Division; you can find another job somewhere."

With that said, he walked away from me, perhaps sensing the emotions that had built up within me.

What the hell? I could "find another job somewhere." My next thought was to chase him down and tackle him for giving me a sucker punch to the gut. We were friends! I had come on board at his request to help him, turning down several other offers because of his coaxing. Justin's actions were clear: It was time to fend for myself.

...

Banking On A Big Pay Day – March 2019

It was a cold morning in New Jersey. The van's windows were frosty, so I removed the scraper from the back of the vehicle to clear the windows. It was hard to believe that it was March. I headed to the garage to get my day's schedule. It would be an easy day. One person from the West Side needed to go to Newark Airport. I hoped my passenger would be nice. An easy ride without any problems would be a nice change.

I saw a young black man approach the van. He was well dressed, wearing a sporty red Nike sweatsuit. I found it funny that he asked, "How do I look?"

"You look great. People seldom leave Fort Dix dressed so nice."

I wasn't lying. Nico got in the van, careful not to spoil his look with needless wrinkles. As we pulled off, he asked,

"How long is the ride?"

I told him it would take a little over an hour. Nico's animated hands and facial expressions emphasized his words as he spoke.

He replied, "After five years in prison, a little over an hour isn't bad."

I took this opportunity to ask what he had done to land in prison. Nico got comfortable in his seat and told me what had happened.

"I was doing all right," he said. "I had a job cleaning offices. I liked it. The money wasn't great, though. My friends were in the same boat, always short on cash. They came up with this plan to rob a bank. I didn't know anything about it. I was going to school. I wasn't learning much, but I was going. I was good at sports. Nah, I was superstar good, man! I played football and basketball. I'm pretty sure the teachers passed me because I played sports. I couldn't read or write. I still can't. Anyway, my friends had this plan about the bank. They were one guy short, so they told me about it. I listened. They were my friends. In the end, I agreed to help with the robbery. They were pretty damn convincing."

I listened intently as Nico continued.

"The plan was to hit a bank in South Boston. It was four of us. One guy was supposed to be the driver. Two guys would rob the bank. I was the fourth. My job was to walk away with the money. They gave me a waiting spot and said they would bring the money to me. All I had to do was walk down the street with it. No one would connect me to the robbery because I wasn't there. You feel me?"

I nodded.

"I'll never forget that day. It was brutal outside. It was cold and wet, with so much *freezen* rain. I was about three blocks away from the bank. I ran the plan through my head over and over. Two guys go into the bank with a fake gun. They demand the money be put in a bag and leave. They'd run around the block and jump in the getaway car parked at the corner. They drive a couple of blocks to me and drop the bag. I put the bag of cash in my backpack and walk; I just keep walking. I was ready."

Nico paused. I took my eyes off the road momentarily to turn in his direction. He was shaking his head as if replaying the events in his head. He continued.

"The robbery went off without a hitch." He exclaimed, "They got the money!"

Nico had just served five years in prison. That was not the end of the legend. "Then what?"

"They left the bank and ran up the block. They said they could hear the bank alarms going off. They said they ran as fast as they could. Then, guess what?"

"What?" I inquired, eager to hear the inevitable turn of events.

Nico said, "No car, damn car!"

I repeated. "No car!" he confirmed.

"I don't know if the driver parked in the wrong place or if he got scared and left, but he was not where he was supposed to be."

Nico shook his head as if he still couldn't believe the driver was f..in M-I-A.

"They called me on the phone and told me to run to 8th Street, saying it wasn't too far from where I was. They said they would meet me there and hand over the cash. I took off running. But remember, it's crazy cold outside. As I was running, I lost one of my sneakers. I didn't let that stop me; I just kept going. Imagine, I'm running down the street in the freezing rain, a black kid wearing a black hoodie and only one sneaker in this Irish neighborhood."

Nico shook his head again, this time with a distinct smirk of disbelief. I wanted to laugh, not at him, but at the image of him running one foot shoeless in the bitter winter cold.

He said, "I met up with my friends. They gave me the bag. Then, we all took off in opposite directions. I was wet, cold, and confused. This was not my neighborhood. I got turned around when they moved me from my original location to 8th Street. When they gave me the bag, I just took off running. I didn't know which direction I was heading. I just ran!"

I correctly predicted that at this point in his recounting, Nico and his one sneaker were about to run into trouble.

"After a couple of blocks, I stopped running. I had to catch my breath and figure something out. This old guy, probably sixty, approached me and asked if I was lost. Before I could say anything, he said, 'And where is your other shoe?' I was out of breath and didn't know what to say anyway. Before I could react, the guy called the police. I started to run again. As soon as I turned the next corner, five police cars were waiting for me. You know how the drama ends. I was holding $6,000 of stolen bank money. It wasn't worth it! Worse decision ever.'"

At this point, Nico was tearing up. His regret was palpable. He told me the two friends who robbed the bank were also caught and charged. The driver wasn't charged. Nico said the driver was nowhere near the bank when the robbery occurred. He said his mistake ruined his life. He can't read or write and now has a federal criminal record. He was under no pretense; he recognized that the road ahead would not be easy. As planned, I dropped Nico off at Newark Airport and wished him good luck. He was heading to Ohio to live with his parents. His story made me wonder how he would find a way to bring order back to his life. Society does not look favorably on felons. It might as well be a scarlet letter hung around his neck in capital letters, *Felon*!

Chapter 5 – Running From The Red – April 2013

I didn't tell Annie about the sale of Aéropostale until after Thanksgiving. She wasn't happy with me hiding such an important thing from her, but she understood that our family deserved to enjoy the holiday without worry. My feelings of anger hadn't changed; I was still pissed about the barebones information received following our overseas trip. A few days after we returned from Hong Kong, Macy's officially informed our team that it planned to sell Aéropostale. Months later, in August 1998, the brand was sold to Bear Stearns for what I thought was a fraction of its worth: $9 million in cash and $9 million in debt. *How is an investment banking firm going to operate a retail apparel brand?* My concerns weren't without reason. On a positive note, everyone kept their jobs, and my *dear friend* was made CEO, a position that included a significant stake in the company.

Aéropostale under Bear Stearns faced as many problems, if not more, than it did under Macy's. Without the support of the Macy's brand, the company struggled to secure lines of credit from vendors necessary to supply merchandise. A group of us had developed strong personal relationships with some vendors. These relationships were cultivated over the years, and we leveraged them to help Aéropostale obtain merchandise. While this was beneficial for the company, I didn't appreciate the near-suffocating weight it placed on us. Key vendors ultimately expected a certain amount of business. After all, everyone in the fashion industry, like every garment, has an angle. Justin was content to oversee the situation and keep the Bear Stearns investor satisfied with what he could gather from our progress.

    I called upon a core group of vendors who had helped make my product line, *In the Paint* brand, a success. Their products were of excellent quality. The pressure to make the company profitable was like carrying a car on my back. Getting things right was the smart thing to do. Despite everything, one thing was clear: Bear Stearns was interested in the bottom line, which had to be profitable.

    I secured a supply of new merchandise with unprecedented delivery schedules for

Aéropostale. The work to revive the company was stressful, but with the vendors' help, our progress was evident, and Aéropostale became a promotional brand. Things were turning around, and my hard work did not go unnoticed. Changes began with the management team. I was promoted to Head Merchant, overseeing all the merchants, designers, and production. It was an exciting and hectic time.

We were a year into the turnaround as we built the Aéropostale brand around the image of a blue-collar family's teen; it wasn't glamorous, but it made a lot of money. The turning point in the company's success was the graphic tee business. Our promotional strategy involved placing men's and women's tees on tables and promoting them as *2 for $20 deals*. The price point was unprecedented at the time, and it worked. You couldn't walk into a mall without seeing a young person with Aéropostale branded across their chest. The graphic tee business was instrumental to Aéropostale's success, and I fought to ensure we didn't alter the winning formula.

I enjoyed my work, and Annie enjoyed hers as a bond trader at First Albany. We were busy, but we made time for our relationship and family. I fell short in this regard more than she did. There were rumors that Aéropostale might go public, and the thought of this was exciting. I was hyper-focused on ensuring Aéropostale's success. It helped being surrounded by colleagues I liked—smart and creative people who became my friends. Time with them was enjoyable. We were coming into our own, proving to the competition that we could capture a piece of the market. In my struggle for work-life balance, work often tipped the scales. I worked constantly. Then, something happened that prompted me to reevaluate my priorities, at least temporarily: the tragedy of September 11, 2001.

    Annie and I were both at work in New York City that day. We took the train, as usual. My office was in the garment district in Midtown Manhattan, while Annie worked in the evolving financial district at 1 Penn Plaza, above Penn Station. I was in a meeting discussing real estate options for a new store when the first plane hit the World Trade Center. We had a television in our conference room that we used to keep up with the news.

Initially, we thought it was a small plane that had hit the building accidentally. Then, when the second plane struck, there was no denying it: it was a terrorist attack. That was the moment I called Annie. All the phone lines were busy. I was worried sick since Annie worked on the 42nd floor of her building. I later learned that she had seen the World Trade Center burning. Shanna also worked in that area of downtown; my heart skipped a beat when we connected by phone. Hearing my daughter's voice provided a bit of comfort during a time of heightened anxiety. Wanting her near me, I told Shanna to come to my office. On the news, the mayor announced that he was shutting the city down. No one would be allowed entry or exit. That was when people in my office started to panic. Some immediately left the building, while I stayed and continued to try to reach Annie. After repeated attempts, I was able to get through. A huge sense of relief washed over me. My wife was okay. She was crying hysterically, but she was safe. I told her to come to my office, assuring her that Shanna was alright and also on her way.

I had tremendous difficulty trying to calm Annie when she reached me. She had friends who worked in the World Trade Center and feared they would not make it out. As the television footage showed the towers' collapse, she froze as her fears were warranted. In the next few hours following the attacks, people covered in soot walked up Broadway and 7th Avenue like zombies. We took water to hand out on the street, hoping it would help.

Around 7 pm, the city was able to move again. The three of us caught the train to Long Island to return home. On the train, strangers hugged and discussed the events of the previous hours, still in disbelief.

Over the following months, the shock of two planes hitting the Twin Towers settled into a harsh reality. Annie and I, along with New York and the whole country, would never be the same. Annie lost many friends that day. With time, a spirit of resilience emerged. Did the rest of the country understand what New York had endured? It reinforced what we all know but often take for granted—that your life can change in an instant. Yet, something else occurred. A cloud of mistrust hung over the city.

Slowly, things in the city returned to normal, and work resumed. Before long, I was back in the thick of it. Aéropostale's growth consumed my thoughts day and night. I was dedicated to improving the brand. Some of my colleagues shared this dedication, and we all worked hard, but others didn't pull their weight. The latter group frustrated me. The company's leadership also lacked clear direction. Too many people are fixated on the potential public offering and the big payday it could bring. This idea made Justin and others more arrogant than ever. Above all, I just wanted Aéropostale to succeed. I wanted the industry to respect the brand I had helped build so far. Thinking they *needed* me was a foolish mistake; more than likely, it was the other way around.

As Justin wrapped up his testimony, I reflected on our friendship. Like everything else, it had changed, dissolving into a cloud of confusion and mistrust.

...

The Three Bears - April 2018

The pick-up was on the West Side. Three men were heading home. One person needed to go to the airport in Philadelphia, while the others were heading to the bus station. I have already been to the bus station four times this week. The same homeless guy who thought I was an FBI agent greeted me each time. It seemed a good bet he would be there again today.

My passengers seemed to be in a rush. They came out quickly and got into the van. One asked me if we could stop so he could get some food. I explained that stopping wasn't allowed. He wanted to know why. Given how the conversation started, this is likely to be one of the more profanity-filled chats.

"Those are the rules. Once you exit the van, you can do what you want."

His face spoke volumes, and he didn't like my response. He was getting agitated, so I asked the two other men to talk to him. With their encouragement, he calmed down.

It was a nice day, and the traffic was light. I estimated that the drive to the bus station would take about forty minutes based on the speed and traffic. I warned the guys not to be alarmed when we arrived, explaining that they might hear someone yelling, "FBI, FBI." You can expect this guy to create a commotion to draw attention. They nodded and seemed content to drive in silence, which was uncommon for most released inmates. When we reached the bus station, we were greeted by the homeless man yelling at me.

"He's the FBI. He's coming to get us."

Two exited the van and headed to the station entrance, including the malcontent.

"We're off to the airport," I told the remaining passenger. He didn't respond. "Are you okay?

His response was somber, "Yeah."

It took him a while to open up and talk.

"I'm Lee. I served in the military and was stationed in Colorado at the air base. I worked in air traffic control and decided the military would be a great training ground. I met a woman who worked as an air traffic controller. She was an Air Force Lieutenant who was smart and beautiful."

He admitted that he was attracted to her at first sight.

"Some guys were intimidated by her rank and good looks. I wasn't. We fell in love and got married. We planned to leave the military. She was good at her job, and the pay was decent. She landed a position as an air traffic controller at a local airport. I got a job as a logistics supervisor for a major freight carrier. We started a family. Within a few years, we had three children. Our lives became more stressful with each new child."

As Lee talked, I tried to imagine what could have led him to prison, prompting him to explain.

"I worked an overnight shift and needed something to help me stay awake. It's hard when no one is around and you haven't slept well. I got my doctor to prescribe a common SSRI that is used to treat depression disorders. It's a serotonin inhibitor."

I quickly began to realize where this was heading.
I was using them every day. I needed them to stay alert and do my job. One day, my doctor said he wouldn't prescribe any more to me. I got desperate. My life was falling apart. I didn't know what to do, even though I knew damn well that surviving without a jolt was impossible.

"What did you do?" My experiences with driving inmates made me expect the answer.

"I asked around and found a local drug dealer who offered to have me sell the pills for him. I sold 'em, and I used 'em. Cliché, huh?"

I didn't respond, thinking it was a rhetorical question.

He said, "I know I screwed up."

"I take it you got busted?".

Lee said, "*Yeah*, after six months of *sellen*. I was *payen* for my use and made some big bucks, too."

Lee told me that he was busted as part of a DEA multi-state operation. He pled guilty and took a plea deal. Sadly, he said, his wife and kids moved to a new place and stopped visiting him in prison long ago.

As we approached the airport, Lee said, "And now?"

I finished his sentence for him, "And now you start over."

Fort Dix and other prisons are full of people like Lee. People start using drugs, prescription and otherwise, and get addicted. Sometimes, that addiction makes them start selling drugs to feed their habit. In prison, some of them are still addicted. On multiple occasions, I have gone into the bathroom area and witnessed men convulsing on the floor, curled up like a dying bug because they were high on bad drugs that were smuggled in. While a resident, I've met firemen, utility workers, police officers, construction men, and others who fell victim to drug use because of an injury or workplace stress. Before this *experience*, it never dawned on me that a painkiller could be a potential gateway drug; I certainly never imagined that so many men would end up selling the drugs that they used. I'm happy that this wasn't my situation, but still stuck in this rotten place.

Chapter 6 – Spinning A Tale – April 2013

The prosecution called its next witness to the stand. It was like watching my life on display before me. Only it was narrated by a nemesis I didn't know existed. My mind drifted to avoid what was about to be said.

    I remembered when the rumors and excitement grew throughout Aéropostale. Plans were made for store expansions, and everyone speculated about how things would change if we went public. It would be great for everyone, but we would have to run the business differently. Then, it happened. We got the news; it was official. The company went public within four years of Bear Stearns' purchase of Aéropostale on May 16, 2002. It was an exciting day for all of us. Our excitement grew as the stock kept climbing, closing at $25. Everyone was ecstatic. Bear Stearns made a billion dollars that day. It was an American success we could all take credit for creating. Aéropostale was a 'real' company, no longer the ugly duckling of the industry. That day, many lives changed.

There was no step-by-step manual to assist us with the transition. After Aéropostale went public, the plan was to open 100 stores each year for five years. There wasn't enough time to read books on navigating the new red waters. We would have to rely on a learning process on the job, with successes and mistakes happening on the same day.

Justin retained his position as CEO. It wasn't a surprise that he was selected to continue leading the company. However, I was shocked by how the announcement transformed him. Or maybe it was the money that changed him. Many of us became wealthy when Aéropostale went public. Our CEO's wealth grew several times more than he could have imagined.

I was promoted to Chief Merchandising Officer and Executive Vice President. In this position, my responsibilities included selecting merchandise for the selling floors and ensuring they were the right products at the right price. One of the competitors we followed was Old Navy. They had great key items and attractive prices. They were expanding their store count and were always busy. Old Navy offered a half-zippered poly fleece for men and women that caught my eye. I purchased several of them and studied them at length. Their popularity looked promising, so I had our manufacturers alter the styling for the Aéropostale brand and make some for us to sell as a Black Friday key item. We placed the new merchandise on presentation tables in front of the stores during the holiday season to encourage the customers to come inside. It was a big hit. Stores that opened at 5 am sold out of their fleece pullovers by 8 am. It was incredible. We were on a roll and not going to look back. We worked hard to ensure that we had products that were on trend. This was essential - the analysts would comment on everything we offered. They would define success or death. We began to earn industry respect and grew our brand and store at a steady rate. We celebrated hitting our milestones, including the lofty goal of opening 100 stores in a year.

Each success we had was met with a new urgency to do more. The demand to hire employees was constant. Finding qualified people with the right customer focus was another stress factor. Sometimes, to my displeasure, we rehired people who had left the company years before when it was failing. I had serious concerns with this practice, not wanting them to reap the benefits of the company they once abandoned. Still, the work had to be done. I tried to stay focused on the positive things, and there were many. For one, I no longer needed to worry about money. Unfortunately, the old saying is true: *money can't buy everything.*

I would have gladly given up all the money from Aéropostale's going public to have been able to save my dad. He became terminally ill with small-cell lung cancer a year after Aéropostale went public. We never saw it coming, and his illness significantly affected my family. He had been my family's strong patriarch and advisor. When he passed away in 2004, everyone from Aéropostale attended his funeral. Their support was unexpected, leaving me unable to find the words to express my gratitude.

After my father, Leonard Finazzo, passed away, I should have left Aéropostale. I had accomplished my goals, but regretted the time it took away from my family. Like most things, the teams were changing with the influx of new people; they wanted a "newness" that was unnecessary. The company's expansion meant entertaining both good and bad ideas. New hires from other teen retailers struggled to adjust to a promotional brand, which created chaos in the company. It was difficult to get everyone on the same page.

    The leadership, including Justin, was changing too. He was my friend, whom I respected, but he had become increasingly demanding. With his growing demands came blossoming arrogance, and at times, his tone was blatantly rude. I didn't like his behavior toward me or others. Money can change you, but not all changes are for the better. Despite my feelings, I continued to do my job to the best of my ability, but there was no denying that my attitude toward work had shifted. It was no longer fun. The thought of leaving often struck me, but I never did. Something always held me back. Loyalty to Aéropostale, the team, and, yes, to Justin froze the intentions. We had bonded. My goal was always to make Aéropostale profitable and successful; that never changed.

    A lot was happening, and all the moving parts concerned me. My preference is for things to be simple and straightforward; they were anything but. Colleagues were having affairs, using drugs at work, and becoming more and more complacent. The mounting pressure from our vendor structure to provide more business as we opened additional stores felt like trying to tow a tractor-trailer. I should have pushed back, but I didn't because some of them were friends. Not only that, I had solicited their help back when Aéropostale didn't have the necessary credit lines; they came through for us when others turned us away. These vendors had supported us in the past; how could I refuse them? My sense of obligation was exhausting. The senior management team collaborated on the buying process to ensure fairness, which we called finalization. The process required the management team to sit in a room for days, examine each item, decide which vendor would supply the product, and then reach a group decision.

    As I sat in the courtroom, thinking about my work at Aéropostale, I questioned why I had been singled out for simply doing my job. Why was I on trial? It all circled back to that office meeting with my boss, whom I thought was a friend. Could things have been done different? I often reflect on things I wish I had done. My personal character is to help others, even at my own expense.

...

Even Cops Get Stung - June 2019

It's a hot Wednesday in June. At 9 am, it is already 82 degrees outside. Wednesdays are typically busy; this Wednesday is no different. A new CO is running the garage. He seems to be a good guy and is fair to all of us drivers. I'm the only driver working today.

The CO gave me a list of 12 names. I needed to drop off the inmates at Newark Airport, Philadelphia Airport, and the bus station in Trenton. Like all the inmates, this group would want me to make their stop my first. Their eagerness to see their families and friends was palpable. I reviewed the itineraries to determine my routes, ensuring everyone would make their respective departures.

The van was loaded with my new group, and they settled in for the ride. An older guy didn't hesitate to yell at me. He seemed irritated. He called me a cop after I assured him I wasn't, but he kept on. Being badgered wasn't part of the job. I made it clear that if he kept yelling, his trip would end right here within the fenced area. He had a choice: settle down or get out of the vehicle. This warning seemed to quiet him. I had a strong sense that this ride would be filled with colorful language. My instincts proved right, as most comments included volumes of crude street talk.

There was a guy in the front with me who also seemed older. He didn't say much. Upon reaching Trenton, five passengers got out. After verifying that they were in the right place, I headed to the Philly airport. The drive was a quick fifteen minutes. Another six guys got out. My only passenger at this point was the older guy sitting next to me. His drop off was at Newark Airport. The only reason he was flying out of Newark instead of Philly was that the flight from Newark was cheaper. I told him we had an hour and forty minutes to drive. His flight departed at 5 pm, so we had plenty of time. We started to chat.

"My name is Don. I'm going to North Carolina, where I was a cop.

Don was a big guy, *the strong and silent type.* There was something about him that just screamed "cop." After learning that he only received a six-month sentence, I asked him what he had done to end up in prison.

"I was a cop in Goldsboro, North Carolina. In the town where I worked, we'd get a lot of calls for domestic disputes. One night, I got a call to respond to a house. I had been to that house earlier in the week and was prepared for drama because you come to expect a scene when domestic violence is involved. Usually, I was by myself, and this time was no different. I arrived at the house after midnight. Dispatch informed me that a man and a woman were having issues. I remembered being at this house the previous night. The woman was high on something, but the husband refused to press charges. I thought the same thing would happen again—I'd show up, she'd be irate, and he'd refuse to press charges. But that didn't happen. As I approached the front door, I heard a man screaming, a scream that indicated he was hurt. I knocked on the door. The same woman from the night before opened it. She must have been around six feet tall and weighed about 275 pounds. Again, she was high on something and acting irrationally, so I called for backup. The backup didn't take long to arrive: a commanding officer and two patrolmen. Their presence seemed to irritate the woman further. She started to move toward us, prompting the commanding officer to say, 'Tase her.' I did. I tased her, but she continued coming toward us; the taser didn't seem to have any effect on her."

At this moment, Don took a deep breath. I sensed this rendition was about to take a turn.

He continued. "The two patrolmen drew their guns. I talked to her, trying to calm her down, but it wasn't working. The man was still screaming in the house. He said he was hurt."

Don turned my way again and asked, "What should I have done?"

I didn't respond. I didn't have an answer.

Don continued, "The other officers' guns were drawn. I had already used my Taser, but that wasn't successful. The commanding officer ordered us to shoot. I was thinking, *we don't need to shoot her.* Yes, she was a threat. She was advancing towards us, but we could have moved backward. That was my thought. The patrolmen didn't shoot. The commanding officer proceeded to tase her. He tased her on the head, and she fell hard. The two officers ran into the house; they found the man bleeding. He had stab marks on his arms and hands."

Don's comments confused me. I didn't understand how that incident landed him in prison. "Was the woman okay?".

"Yeah, she was okay. She was rushed to the hospital. She called a civil rights lawyer before she reached home the next day. The commanding officer and I were indicted on a civil rights violation."

I wanted to say, "You didn't do anything wrong," but I held back. I'm not a lawyer. Don said he lost his job. He took a plea deal, which resulted in his six-month sentence. He mentioned the commanding officer got 19 months in federal prison.

He asked me, "What did I do wrong? I kept her from getting shot!"

Justice can be blind, even to the extent of being blind to reality. If what Don described was unembellished, he was another victim of the *Justice System*. The ride took slightly over two hours, but Don still had time to catch his flight home to his wife and children.

Chapter 7 – How Would This End – April 2013

A week into the trial, I couldn't get a read on the jury. My lawyer assured me everything was going well. But the look on Bob's face told me this was his standard response. My family attended court daily; this day was no different. Listening to the testimony was like hearing a replay of my life. The words were like a bad play. At one point, I stopped listening, unable to bear it anymore. This was like picking up on the replay that was still swimming in my head from the day before. The dialog made me recall when I no longer considered my job one of my blessings.

My work made me unhappy, and I didn't know how to deal with these new feelings. Although I was excelling in many ways, misery became my only companion. My thoughts often focused on leaving the company. Everything was changing, and my attention became finding the right time to leave. Annie encouraged me not to wait. "Just leave," she told me. I should have listened to her.

The executives at Aéropostale were constantly vying for higher positions. Money was changing everyone. Requests from Justin and others came as barking orders. Being good at my job, his 'guidance' was unnecessary; our success proved that. I was tired of being told what to do and how to do it, only to feel like my efforts were not enough. Business was good, there were no issues, so what was the point of this micro-management? We had established a niche in the marketplace as a promotional specialty store offering great items at compelling prices. The Aéropostale story was one of success. It was time to enjoy what we had built. Instead, I faced endless questions and persistent sour attitudes. Among all my challenges, my relationship with Justin was the most frustrating. I disapproved of his business approach and resented his demands on me. No matter how many issues I had with him, his wife faced even more.

Justin was showing increased signs of pressure from the job. After years as the top executive, he was struggling with decision-making. He would call me day and night due to the challenges and pressures of his job.

While not fond of it, I always took his calls. Sometimes he would rant about his marriage; other times, he would call to tell me about something with a big price tag he was eyeing. I listened and replied with plenty of "wow," "I get it," and "hang in there."

I started to think about what would happen if Justin's life became more troubled with marital issues. I don't know why my thoughts went there, but they did. This made me want to get my finances in order. Unlike Justin, my beginnings had been modest. I had acquired more money than I had imagined would result from Aéropostale going public, and I was grateful for this. My few investments in real estate had proved lucrative. Nearly all the liquid assets were sitting in the bank. I needed to ensure Annie and the kids would be okay if anything happened to me, which prompted me to consult an estate and trust attorney to get my paperwork in order.

Around this time, Aéropostale was about to open its 700th store in Las Vegas. It was a big deal. The company planned a celebratory dinner at Tao Restaurant Bistro, an exotic Asian restaurant, to mark the occasion. As was my routine, I attended the opening celebration alone. Justin traveled with his son, who was turning sixteen. Everyone was in a good mood that evening, including me. Despite my thoughts of leaving the company, I had worked hard for Aéropostale for 10 years. We grew from 99 stores to 700 in record time. I knew I wouldn't miss this celebration; I had earned it.

  The drinks flowed, the music played, we ate, and had a good time. Justin was in rare form, even for him. Many Aéropostale executives, particularly women, came to me to complain about Justin throughout the evening. They were reacting to his continuous pushing. His constant requests were to do more to give more. Knowing Justin the way I did, his behavior did not surprise me. He was a closet micro-manager. I brushed off the comments, ignoring the woman who had an idea to use his behavior against him. I told myself that it was none of my business. Despite my feelings, Justin was a grown man who would do what he wanted, thinking that his behavior was all for the company's good.

  Before going to bed that night, I called Annie to hear her voice. Our relationship was built on trust. I wanted her to know I was alone in my room, and have her think for a second that Justin and all the stress were changing me. Whether in Vegas or not, I would always remain true to my wife.

Well, the adage goes, *"What happens in Vegas* does not always stay in Vegas." Justin's Vegas behavior was the whispered topic of choice back in the office. His overbearing management style had caused quite a stir in Nevada and friction in the teams. Much to my surprise, weeks after the trip, it had not lessened.

When Justin called me into his office, my first reaction was one of annoyance. *What now?* He told me there would be an internal audit on "us" doing things. This surprised me, and my face must have shown based on Justin's frown. *What was he talking about? There was no us doing things.*

He constantly crossed boundaries, attempting to leverage people to motivate them to work harder. He told me he was being investigated for securing the Real World Suite for his son's birthday. The suite was popular due to its association with the television show *The Real World*, and it was almost impossible to rent. One of Aéropostale's vendors gambled a lot at the Palms Hotel and ensured that Justin got the suite for his son. This wasn't information I needed; I had actual work to do. Justin mentioned that emails across the company would be reviewed as part of the investigation. This did not raise any alarms for me; everything seemed reasonable at the time.

    I have often thought about that day in Justin's office. Nothing struck me as odd then. Justin had perfected his poker face. For the life of me, I can't remember how he turned that conversation into what my involvement was outside of Aéropostale, but he did. He could have said many things to let me know what was happening. He didn't say any of them. He was my friend. We had hiccups in our relationship, but we built something great together. We were both instrumental in making Aéropostale a success. That, more than anything, bonded us. I was wrong.

    The investigation, which presumably began with Justin, turned into an investigation into me. I never saw it coming. There was no email trail about Justin's ability to secure the luxury suite at the Palms. However, an email in my inbox generated interest.

It turned out that the estate attorney I used to get my paperwork in order accidentally sent an email detailing my finances to my Aéropostale email instead of my personal email. The email disclosed my net worth, including my real estate holdings. This was a big deal, as it showed that some of my real estate holdings were acquired through corporations I owned with an Aéropostale vendor, Doug, who was one of the t-shirt manufacturers. From the outside, this could appear to be a conflict of interest and bribes. I didn't feel a conflict existed because there was nothing involved other than an independent real estate deal with this vendor, who was both someone Aéropostale had as a vendor and a personal friend; the two were mutually exclusive.

I met this vendor in the early 1990s. He manufactured T-shirts for the Arcade Shop at Macy's Herald Square. I was trying to make progress with my *In the Paint* brand, and Doug owned a print shop on Long Island. He was introduced to me as someone in the fashion industry who could provide screen printing for T-shirts. We hit it off and built a friendship. And yes, we did business together in fashion and real estate projects. When I started working for Aéropostale, there was an urgent need to bring in new vendors who could handle quick-turn projects. Doug was one of the vendors I invited to meet the team. He became a key part of Aéropostale's graphics side of the business.

It might have seemed like I favored Doug by giving him business, but that was not the case. We needed products, and he offered them at a great price. Justin, I, and many others worked our butts off, and the brand saw significant growth; this increased our demand for products. Yes, our vendors prospered, and everyone's business expanded. Everyone made money. There was nothing shady about it. Unfortunately, my view was in the minority.

Things around the office grew tenser than usual when that email was discovered. I continued to do my job. Justin assured me that everything was fine regarding the investigation into him. I was happy for him. What he didn't tell me was that I was being investigated. The next couple of months were nothing short of strange. My name had replaced Justin's as the topic of gossip.

Something felt off; my inner self sensed it. Justin started communicating very little with me, which was weird. Even weirder was that whenever he spoke up, it was with a silly comment that he always made in front of a group of coworkers.

One day, I was advised I needed to attend a board meeting. This confused me because executives were always given a briefing binder before every board meeting, and I didn't receive one. There were no briefing books that day, but there was a tape. Justin had recorded our conversation the day he called me into his office to discuss the internal audit and our actions. Now it made sense why he asked me about my activities outside of Aéropostale. He was recording my conversation about my real estate holdings. The board listened as the tape played. I was instantly transported back to the time after the planes hit the Twin Towers, and the air of mistrust loomed in the atmosphere. It was suffocating. No one asked for my perspective. I, the Executive Vice President and Chief Merchandising Officer of Aéropostale, was immediately terminated for cause for failing to disclose my real estate holding with a vendor.

My mind swirled. *What the hell just happened?* I left the office in disgrace and disgust. Justin didn't say a word.

...

The Fish Story - October 2019

It's fall. The leaves are changing color. The bright yellow, red, and orange hues match my mood. I'm happy because it's Friday. It's also football season. College football will be on TV tomorrow. The NFL game is on Sunday. Football is a big deal in prison. Most of the guys, including me, look forward to watching the games. Oh yes, one more thing, a lot of betting goes on in prison. Bets are placed on games, on the Super Bowl, and on anything you can think of. There are times when inmates become so indebted, they need to make arrangements to have money sent from home or face painful consequences. This could be the subject of an entire book.

Only one guy was going home today, so my workday was going to be easy. I headed to the East Side to pick him up. Time is an enemy in prison, though none of us here had a choice. My passenger was running late, and I suspected he was delayed waiting for an officer to bring his money. In federal prison, you can earn money by working or having someone outside deposit funds into your commissary account. Any money in your account must be given to you when you leave prison. The process of being *cashed out* usually takes some time.

    A guy was heading my way. He looked to be in his mid-40s. His appearance—what was the word? Unassuming? No. Indifferent? No, that wasn't it. Defeated, I guessed. He got in the car. I asked him where he was going to make small talk. He was going to Penn Station in Philadelphia. He confirmed his destination in a murmur and nod. His tone and sadness when he spoke offered an unexpected view into him. It was a familiar sight. Driving down Route 38, I asked, "How long have you been in?" I was surprised to hear the guy say six months. And was in disbelief at what he said he had done. Curiosity was getting the best of me. "What did you do?" I didn't believe my ears. Six months for what? I asked again, "What did you do?"

    He repeated, "I overfished."

Reflections Of A Town Driver

Yep, that's what I thought he said. At that moment, I'm certain I looked puzzled. Puzzled hardly came close to my thoughts. Someone spent six months in prison for catching more fish than allowed.

"I'm Patrick. I owned a boat, nothing fancy, enough to help me make a living as a fisherman. I owned a business, fishing the waters of Chesapeake Bay. I was caught overfishing in federal waters and pulled over by the Coast Guard. They checked my boat and paperwork. I was thinking this was a routine stop. Things changed when the Coast Guard told me that I had overfished the striped bass. My paperwork stated that I had reached my quota for the season. They charged me with a federal crime. Imagine that: a federal crime for catching too many fish. Not a simple fine. No, they charged me as a felon. I lost my boat, spent six months in federal prison, and had to pay a $100,000 fine."

In my mind, I just kept thinking, *all of this because you caught too many fish?*

I learned that the federal government protects the waters from fishermen who overfish, and it's common for people to be arrested and fined for doing so. Before meeting

Patrick, I had never thought that overfishing could result in federal crime charges. Patrick said he made a mistake. He was facing 27 months, but he took a plea deal. His sadness never left his tone as he recounted his situation.

"I have nothing now. No boat, no business, no wife. She left me. I have nothing. This wiped me out, all for catching too many fish. No tons, not dragging a net. Just hard, backbreaking work, and they busted me."

Patrick said he was returning to Maryland to live with his 80-year-old mother. His future was unclear, like murky water. I've known that life can take a person in many directions. People get lost. Some eventually find their way; some don't. His comments were laced with acidic words of a man violated. Patrick took his time getting out of the car when we reached Penn Station. He seemed in no rush to catch his train.

As Patrick disappeared from my sight, all kinds of people landed in federal prison, from drug dealers and murderers to gang members and bank robbers. You think this was a pretty good representation of the residents. Now, a fisherman could be added to the list.

It has been a year since I put this entry in my journal. Now, it needed updating. Another inmate, a good friend of Patrick's, had read a news article from home. Patrick had killed himself. I didn't want to believe it, but the inmate showed me an article. The article said that a fisherman, Patrick, from the Chesapeake Bay area, committed suicide after losing his business and serving time in federal prison. What a sad ending to a situation I wished was fiction. I pray he is resting in peace.

Chapter 8 – Painful Progress – April 2013

The trial had reached its halfway point. My stomach was churning, and an unsettled feeling had taken hold of me. My fate was in the hands of twelve strangers. This feeling wasn't new to me. Remembering the last time I experienced it, I was still at Aéropostale, and my mother had died. That was in June 2006. Losing your parents shakes you to your core. The passing of my mother was harder on me than my father's. It wasn't because I loved her more; my love for them was equal. It was because her departure from Earth meant I was parentless. One might not think a grown man would need his parents, but I did and missed them dearly. Annie and the kids comforted me; I tried to do the same for them. Hiding my pain was unsuccessful, but Annie saw through my attempts. She was a godsend, constantly assuring me that everything would work out and we would be okay. I wanted to believe her.

  I was not feeling great about how the trial was going. Hearing about being fired was triggering. My thoughts again drifted back to being overwhelmed with fear about what the industry would say about me, and that I had been fired. *Would my name and character be tarnished forever?* My concern was that Aéropostale might try to bring a civil suit against me, given that its stock had dropped 15% after the news of my firing was made public. Those worries led me to become depressed. That state of mind lingered for a long time.

After being fired, Aéropostale ceased doing business with the Long Island vendor. This action was devastating to our trusted merchandise provider. The feeling of devastation was familiar. I had planned many retirement parties for colleagues at Aéropostale and had always looked forward to the day it would be my turn. I had hoped to receive the legendary gold watch, but that was now impossible. I was now a pariah.

Sitting in the courtroom gave me time to reflect on my life after leaving Aéropostale. It wasn't easy; work had been a major part of my life. Now, every day was just another day at home. Watching television wouldn't be satisfying; my pride was tied to working. Annie offered all the supportive words I had come to rely on when facing challenges. She never pushed me to "snap out of it." She just loved me. A few close friends from Aéropostale called to check on me, but they made it clear that the company had instructed everyone to have no contact with me. Because of this, their calls were infrequent. Even vendor relationships built over years were afraid to call me. After weeks, Justin called. True to form, his call was to ask for help. Imagine being fired for cause, and the CEO calling for my help. Such a lack of empathy—pure self-interest without a drop of compassion. It seemed this chapter of my life had ended. I understood my situation and began considering *what's next*.

It took me over a year to become tired enough of being miserable to take action. This newfound energy was sparked by the arrival of my first grandchild, Valentina, who was born just before my difficult work upheaval. Her presence in my life helped me gain a better perspective. It was time for me to find a new job and start living again. I have good instincts, which are vital for success as a fashion merchant. From my experience in retail, I learned how important it is to stay current and to distinguish between trends and fads; my gut and experience helped me to tell them apart. Despite what happened with Aéropostale, I remained hopeful about continuing to work in this field. Still, was my reputation before my firing enough to outweigh the dark stain left on my reputation?

My concerns about being blackballed in the industry were put to rest when a friend informed me that Sun Capital was seeking a head merchant for Anchor Blue, a struggling retail company it owned. Anchor Blue was previously owned by Miller's Outpost and sold a variety of trendy denim items, including both California brands and private labels. It had some of the same issues Aéropostale had in its early days: bleeding cash.

I left home on a Monday morning to meet with Anchor Blue's president. The office was in Ontario, California, a few hours north of Los Angeles. The majestic, snow-capped mountain that overlooked the office made up for the long flight and subsequent drive.

The days were planned to include meetings with the people I would be working with and a session with the president. The meeting with the president was eye-opening. My first impression of Tom was that he was a great guy. It wasn't lost on me that he seemed very different from my previous boss. He was calm, polite, and well-liked. It was clear from the earlier meeting that his team respected him as a leader. The culture had a palpable vibe of positivity, unlike the privileged, rude, and competitive atmosphere of Aéropostale.

The next day's schedule included meetings with several key staff members. They were smart, laid-back, and genuinely interested in growing the company. I could see myself working well with them. I called Annie from the hotel to tell her about my day and mentioned that I would meet the rest of the Anchor Blue team the following day. Sleep was refreshing that night.

As planned, the second day involved meeting additional staff. We discussed the differences between East Coast and California customers and how I could help the company reach its expansion goals. The president was pleased with my pitch and my work at Aéropostale. Sun Capital hired me to address the issues. Since they were based on the West Coast, I had to travel between New York and

California. After the Aéropostale debacle, the laid-back attitude of Californians suited me. It didn't take long to get back into the groove. Traveling coast to coast was not an issue.

At Anchor Blue, we combined California style with private labels and implemented plans to make every store look uniform. Customers were attracted by promotional tables placed at each store's entrance, and we expanded the denim selection for both men and women. I wasted no time calling vendors who had helped me at Aéropostale to work for Anchor Blue. Each delivered updated products, and Anchor Blue launched a private label. Although our relationship changed with a previous key vendor, he had moved on and started a new company. This contact became one of Anchor Blue's important vendors. I hoped this would rekindle my previous relationship, but it didn't, at least not to the same level. Some companies we worked with always wanted more; nothing was ever enough for them. Working with others again, however, gave me a sense of continuity and purpose. I felt renewed enthusiasm, similar to when we built Aéropostale.

As the months passed, everyone at Anchor Blue could see we were on the right track and headed for growth. All the signs were pointing to the company succeeding. As the business grew, private equity groups began to evaluate our performance. They had their own way of looking at things and determining what was best. Ultimately, a decision was made for the company to file Chapter 11 to restructure—a planned bankruptcy. I, along with other key players, was tasked with pulling Anchor Blue out of bankruptcy, with the hope of taking the company public.

Within two years of working at Sun Capital, I helped revive Anchor Blue after it filed for Chapter 11. As a reward, I was promoted to Executive Vice President. I was back at the top of my game, and plans were in motion for a public offering a reality. That all came to an end when the FBI showed up at my house to arrest me for violating the Travel Act. I did the right thing by resigning.

I didn't know it then, but the vendor I had worked with on some real estate was also charged. He was able to surrender to the FBI; that courtesy was not extended to me. He was aware of the situation, but, as is often the case with matters like this, he was advised not to communicate with me. I understood that. In situations like this, people in such predicaments try to mitigate damage to another person. It seemed that this may have occurred in this case as well. My former friend and partner accepted a plea deal of four and a half years in prison. When he made that decision, our friendship came to an end.

    The judge struck his gavel, snapping me out of my daydream. The prosecution called its next witness. It was clear that each witness had been expertly instructed on how to respond and what to say. Innocent actions, like breaking a pencil in a meeting, were twisted to portray me as an angry, fear-provoking boss. I listened in dismay, praying that somehow the jury would clear me of all charges. The expert witness my lawyers wanted to put on the stand, a professor from Tulane University, was not allowed to testify. Had my case been strong enough to counter the misrepresentations presented by the other side? I had debated whether to take the stand and share my version of events, but decided against it. My fate was left in the hands of 12 strangers.

After only five hours of deliberation, the jury reached its verdict. The charges consisted of one count of conspiracy to commit mail and wire fraud and violate the Travel Act, as well as fourteen counts of mail fraud and one count of wire fraud. I stood steadfast as the judge read the special verdict the jury rendered.

"On the conspiracy count, the jury finds Mr. Finazzo guilty of conspiracy to commit mail fraud based on intent to deprive Aéropostale of the right to control the use of its assets. On count two, the jury finds Mr. Finazzo guilty of conspiracy to commit wire fraud based on Aéropostale's right to control the use of its assets, but not on the intent to deprive Aéropostale of money. On each of the fourteen substantive mail fraud counts and the wire fraud count, the jury finds Mr. Finazzo guilty of denying Aéropostale's right to control the use of its assets, but not based on intent to deprive Aéropostale of money."

What did all of this mean? By my best estimation, according to the law, as judged by my 'peers,' I was guilty of something, and something became guilty of everything. They claimed I took away Aéropostale's right to make decisions. This made no sense to me because Aéropostale hired me to make decisions for the company. There was no need to turn around to know that Annie was in tears.

I left the courthouse with my family and friends. So many people had come to support me, and I was grateful they were there. The presence of Annie, my children, sisters, brother-in-law, nieces, nephews, and dear friends helped me put on a brave face. We didn't stick around after the guilty verdicts were announced. I was exhausted from the trial and all the lies about me, and I just wanted to get home.

After many failed attempts, I finally perfected my poker face. The press waited for my reaction, but I gave none. We all got into our cars, parked across the street at Cadman Plaza, and headed home. The pressure of waiting for the verdict was gone; now, I had to focus on what was coming next.

My sentencing date was set for August 2014, over a year after the verdict. I spent most of that time with my family, trying to enjoy every moment we could. Silently, I was angry at myself for the mess that we were living through. I was going to prison, and there was no doubt about that. The only question was how long. I often thought about a song by Coldplay called *Trouble*, "They spun a web for me."

Chapter 9 – A New Reality – August 2014

On the morning of my sentencing, I felt numb. The August heat was oppressive, and so was my mood. A year after the verdict, the thought of the fate awaiting me was unshakeable. I tried to distance myself from life and family because it hurt too much. One consequence of the stress was the expansion of my waist. Thirty uninvited pounds rested there while at home, lying around and not working, waiting for this day to arrive. The day of reckoning had come; there was no avoiding it. A twisted sense of relief washed over me. Now my family no longer had to deal with constant court dates, weekend calls from attorneys, and finger-pointing. No one should have to go through this torturous drama.

My instincts told me that the judge and jury never really got to know me as a *person*. The entire situation was upsetting. As the Coldplay song says, I was in trouble for "all the stupid things I said... all the stupid things I'd done." I had caused pain and shame for my family. We spoke very little that day, but I had an important conversation with my seven-year-old granddaughter, Valentina. Telling her business required me to go to China, and she wouldn't be able to see me for a while. The truth was, I was given 60 days to report to Fort Dix, a converted military base from the 1960s in New Jersey that now operates as a low-security federal prison for male offenders. The judge's order was for eight years for substantive mail and wire fraud counts and five years for the conspiracy count, to run concurrently. The sentence also included three years of supervised release and a $13 million restitution order.

Supervised release is another way for the government to extend your sentence. You are required to check in with your supervised release officer in person, over the phone, or via FaceTime. If you want to go to the grocery store, get a haircut, or visit a friend, you need to get permission.

There are many stages of supervised release; you must wear an ankle bracelet during this part of your sentence. Check in with the officer assigned to you every day. Everyone is treated equally without empathy. You can violate the Travel Act, sell drugs, or rob a bank; we all face the same consequences.

    At 5 am on October 14, 2014, I left my family—my wife, daughter, sister, and niece—all crying in our living room, walking out our door for what would be the last time for several years. My emotions were overwhelming. Their suffering is as distressing as any part of the *memorable*. Moreover, I hated that the burden of what was happening was due to my actions. Exiting like an escaped POW to evade my suffocating sense of guilt.

    My son, Tony, and two male in-laws drove me to surrender myself. We stopped at Exit 7 on the New Jersey Turnpike to grab a bite. My last meal in the free world, at least for the foreseeable future, was a breakfast plate from Denny's. We kept the conversation positive, with them reassuring me that I would be home soon. We all hoped that would be true. I refused to feel sorry for myself or accept any pity from them. My only concern, my only worry, was Annie. I asked my son to look after her, and he promised he would; it was the only way I could get through this ordeal. After eating, we drove another twenty minutes before reaching Fort Dix.

Unaware of where to go, the visiting room lobby felt like a good choice. The officer on duty looked up from her paperwork and said, "The visiting hours have been delayed because of a problem in the yard."

She immediately went back to her task. I told her I was not a visitor.

"I'm here to check in." It probably sounded like I was checking into a hotel.

The officer glanced at me again. "On a Saturday?" she asked.

No one, not my lawyer or the prison consultant I hired, told me that prisoners are not supposed to self-surrender on the weekend.

The correctional officer said, "Wait here, I have a place for you."

An hour later, after waiting, I was escorted to the entry area and strip-searched. I was given a pair of pants, a T-shirt, a blanket, and a rubber mattress. The next stop was the Special Housing Unit, or the SHU (pronounced shoe), as it's called. It didn't take long to realize I had been placed in solitary confinement. For the next 48 hours, my surroundings was the SHU, where my only companion was my sour thoughts. The cell contained a toilet and a sink for washing. Food was delivered through a tray pushed through a hole in the door. Confused and afraid that this would be my home for the next eight years, I found that to be a horrifying thought.

Those two days in the SHU were the worst of my life. On Monday afternoon, I was transferred to the Camp, the lowest-level prison facility. Compared to the SHU, it seemed like a five-star hotel. This marked the start of the journey that would ultimately lead me home.

Paradise Lost - January 2010

I'm not looking forward to the cold air this morning. It's snowing outside, but like the post office, I must deliver my *package* today. Only one guy is leaving, so at least the day's drive won't be too long in the inclement weather.

The CO instructed me to drop off the released inmate at the Philadelphia airport. He said his flight was in the afternoon, so I didn't need to rush. I turned on the heat to warm the van and waited patiently for the guy to come out of the prison. When he stepped outside, he was wearing shorts. I couldn't understand why he didn't wear warmer clothes, but I didn't see it as my concern. Clothes other than the green uniform provided to inmates have to be purchased. Some guys don't have the money to buy much clothing; the shorts might have been the best clothing my passenger owned.

The CO handed the guy off to me, and he got in the van. I asked him to buckle up before putting the van in drive. He fastened his seat belt and introduced himself.

"I'm Campbell," he said.

"I'm Finazzo. Where are you from, Campbell?"

"Me, I was born in Jamaica, but I've been in the States for years."

Campbell told me he was at Fort Dix for 33 months, his final stop after being at several other prisons. In total, he spent nine and a half years in prison. Campbell said he was heading to Florida to stay with a cousin in Gainesville.

"What landed him in prison?"

Campbell took a deep breath and explained. I tried to focus on the icy road while listening.

"I grew up in the United States, but I love my Jamaica. I was educated here. I did good in school. My dad died when I was barely 20. Nothing was the same after that. My sister lives in Jamaica. She was dating a guy who traveled back and forth between the two countries. One day, her boyfriend suggested that I *holler* out to a friend of his. He said he could hook me up with some work. I needed the money. After my dad died, I was responsible for supporting my family. We talked, and you know, that's how I got into the drug game."

Without replying, I nodded my head. The snow was falling sideways and sticking to the windshield. Campbell kept going,

"I smuggled drugs for years. I would fly to Jamaica, pick up the stuff, and bring it back. I was good at it. I did it for years! I got pretty girls to work for me, and they would bring some in, too. We would split up, entering through different airports, then meet at a central location a few days later. The group I worked for kept asking me to make more and more trips. It was becoming too much, so I decided it was time to get out of the business. It was on my last trip when I got caught."

Campbell didn't say it expressly, but from the way he explained what he did, I concluded that he smuggled the drugs in by swallowing them and then later purging them from his body. He said the DEA and the Department of Homeland Security arrested him as he came through customs. He refused to provide information about the group he worked for, as doing so would mean certain harm to his family. When Campbell finished describing his situation, he was shaking. I wasn't sure if he was cold or still affected by the thoughts of what he had done. Pulling up to the airport, Campbell said, "My wife, mother, and sister are in Jamaica."

He lowered his head and continued.

"I'll never be able to visit them again. Going back would have serious consequences for me and them."

Chapter 10 – Introductions – August 2014

An inmate named Dan welcomed me upon arriving at the camp. He stood six feet tall, had an average build, and looked to be around my age. He also, dare I say, was friendly. He invited me to sit and chat. He chuckled when I mentioned spending the previous two days in solitary confinement, prompting him to share the lay of the land with me. I appreciated his insights and wanted to learn everything I could to avoid being caught off guard. Dan explained that Fort Dix Prison was a low-security facility. My lawyer had told me that, but I didn't interrupt him.

"The prison complex has an East Side and a West Side; in the middle of the two is this mess called a satellite prison camp, aka *The Camp*."

That's where I was housed. Inmates like me who had been found guilty of non-violent or white-collar crimes might serve their entire sentences here if they were under ten years. Other inmates who committed violent crimes and were nearing their release date would also be housed here to help transition back into society. Unlike the East and West Sides, which had more restrictive living arrangements, the Camp offered open military dormitory-style living. Inmates all slept in one of two large rooms, in bunk beds lined back-to-back. Despite this difference, I soon learned that in prison, little distinction is made between inmates. With a few exceptions, a murderer and an embezzler are treated the same. I also learned that this place was not without danger.

    Hearing Dan speak confirmed that I was no longer in control of my life. The next few years would be shared with 300 to 400 other men. You have to use communal showers and toilets, sit in the same spot for meals because that was an unspoken rule, and do as you're told. Now I was not the person in charge. Decisions would be made for me, and I would have to accept that. There was no alternative.

    Dan introduced me to a couple of guys who were nice to me. To sum them up, they seemed like good men who had made poor decisions. I'm sure some bad people were in the camp (in time, this thought proved to be an accurate assumption), but that didn't matter because we were all just numbers. We were all in the same messy boat, living under the same challenging circumstances.

I took an empty bottom bunk in the middle of the room. Bottom bunks were preferred, and residents strove to get one. I tried to convince myself that sleeping next to and beneath other men was no different from being at a boys' summer camp. Still, it didn't do much to allay my anxiety. I tried to size up all the men who would be my roommates without appearing too obvious. Every race and ethnicity imaginable was represented; it was like a United Nations of criminals. There was also a range of ages among the men, though most seemed to be over 40. What surprised me most was the presence of "celebrities." Among my roommates were a Grammy Award-winning music producer, a business tycoon, and even a congressman.

The first night at dinner, I sat with Dan and a couple of the other he had introduced me to earlier in the day. It was at dinner that I could see the cliques that existed. I planned to keep my head down and my nose clean. During dinner, Dan asked me what landed me in this hole. I explained my situation to him.

He reciprocated, telling me that he retired from working construction when he had a fall on the job. He was granted disability pay, and the state paid the doctor in charge of his care. Dan said he didn't know it, but the doctor was involved in a disability fraud scheme. The doctor and all his patients were charged.

That night in my bunk, sleep would not come. The mattress was hard, but even harder was accepting the reality of being here. I thought about Annie, missing home, sitting next to her. I glanced at the man in the bottom bunk next to me, wondering who he was and what he had done.

No Safe Place - April 2018

Getting away from this place always feels good. The CO told me there were four guys to pick up on the East Side and one on the West Side. He instructed me to go to the East Side first, saying that the West Side was on lockdown, which meant no one could move. This happens on occasion when things go awry. Usually, it's because a fight occurred or contraband, like drugs, a cell phone, or a weapon, was found.

I headed to the East Side, straight to the pick-up spot. It took no time for four guys to come out and get in the van. I was driving a 12-passenger vehicle, so they spread out. They were talking among themselves, and I let them do so without interfering. Next, we headed to the West Side of the complex. After five minutes, the last passenger still had not exited the building. The guys in the van were getting restless; they wanted to get on the road. They urged me to leave without the last passenger, but I could not, explaining that we had to wait. Several minutes later, the CO approached the car. He spoke loud enough for all the guys in the van to hear him.

"He'll be out soon; they have cleared the compound."

As the CO turned from the van, a man was walking toward us. At first, I thought he was wearing a camouflage shirt. Looking closer, I saw his shirt wasn't camouflaged; it was bloodied. My eyes widened. I couldn't imagine why they hadn't allowed him to get cleaned up before heading home. The man also had two bandages on his head, both bloodied. He looked like he was in bad shape. My passengers spoke up immediately when they saw him. They were loud and talking quickly. Each refused to sit next to the last passenger. There was no time to debate them, so I let the guy to sit in the front of the van with me.

The CO yelled to me, "Make sure he's the last drop."

As I pulled off, the guys in the back of the van started yelling at the new passenger. Their comments were colorful. Vile street talk at its best. They called him all sorts of names, none of them good. They only stopped at my request. I told them I couldn't concentrate on the road. If I got into an accident, we would all have to go back to prison. This prompted them to ease up on the insults. I drove the four guys from the East Side to Trenton as fast as possible. From their conversation, it became clear that they were local guys from New York City, New Jersey, and Connecticut. They exited the van in Trenton with a few more choice words for the bloody guy sitting beside me. I was then alone with, if the guys in the back of the van were correct, a pedophile.

Reflections Of A Town Driver

The ride to the Philly bus station on Filbert Street would take about forty minutes. Until now, I hadn't said a word to my last passenger. He seemed very disoriented. I usually waited until there was only one person in the vehicle to start a conversation. I'd ask them what they did to land at Fort Dix and how long they served. Maybe it was out of habit, but I asked despite fearing what might be said.

Well, the guys in the back of the van were right. Phil was a pedophile. In prison, that means you get no respect, and you are likely to be targeted and hurt by the other inmates. That's what happened to Phil the previous night. Phil opened up.

"Last night, I was beaten in the head with locks stuffed in a sock."

The dried blood covering his head, face, and shirt was evidence of his suffering. His constant moaning confirmed it. He was headed back to West Virginia. He might have told me more, but my mind drifted to my granddaughter. The thought of someone abusing her was unbearable. I pressed harder on the gas pedal, eager to reach the bus station in Philly as fast as I could.

When I pulled up to the bus station, my homeless tormentor was there. As usual, when he saw me, he started chanting, "FBI, FBI." It didn't bother me. I parked the van and looked at Phil. His head and face were swollen. He let out a shrieking groan from his injuries. I didn't want to care, but for some reason, the feeling stirred within me. My thought was to tell him to go to hell, but I asked if he had his ticket. He didn't respond. I asked him to get out of the van. He didn't move. I grabbed a pair of blue disposable gloves from the van and put them on. I went around to the passenger side of the van, opened the door, and helped Phil out of the van onto the sidewalk. He had no idea where he was. When I asked him again if he had a ticket, he slowly reached into his black trash bag and pulled out a book, with his ticket sticking out of the pages.

    I considered leaving Phil on the sidewalk and going back to the van. The thought that he was abusing children made me sick, and I felt he didn't deserve help. Still, the Christian in me couldn't ignore that he was badly hurt and needed first aid. I signaled two transit police officers and asked for their help to get

Phil inside. I told them what had happened to Phil, omitting some details. One of them hesitated. The other agreed to help Phil onto his bus. I returned to the van as Phil disappeared into the bus station. Even though he was out of sight, the picture of him and men like him haunted me.

Chapter 11 – It's Never Enough – July 2018

I thought my days inside the courtroom were over; I was wrong. My attendance at the restitution hearing was required—a separate hearing about the amount of money I would have to pay Aéropostale for my *crime* against the company. A jailhouse lawyer had explained everything to me. This lawyer asked if I wanted to file Form 2255, Motion to Get a New Trial. This form is used when a defendant believes they received ineffective counsel during the trial, requesting a new trial. Such a decision would require careful thought on my part. I had accepted my sentence despite my firm belief in my innocence. I couldn't fathom what I did to land me in this situation. A new trial was an unimaginable event. The thought of this hanging over my family for the next few months was not an acceptable prospect. Sparing them any further pain was my highest priority.

    On the day of my restitution hearing, I was shackled for the bus ride to Brooklyn. My humiliation made me want to hide. Never in my life was the possibility of being in this position ever imagined. I was assigned a public defender to act as my counsel; there was no way I would shell out more money on the high-priced firm that had represented me at my trial. My assets were gone. Everything had been taken.

At the courthouse, I was placed in a holding cell with five other men. One of them, a guy from Trinidad, told me he needed to decide whether to testify. He said he only had three hours to make his decision. His trepidation was palpable even through his heavy accent. He told me that if he testified, he or his family would be killed.

In a stressed voice, he said, "Odds are we'd all end up dead."

Unlike the other men in the cell who left and came back, when the guard called for the Trinidadian to leave the cell, he never returned.

When it was time for my restitution hearing, I had already decided not to pursue a new trial and told my public defender to hold off on submitting Form 2255. I went back to Fort Dix, determined to survive the hand life had dealt me.

My first couple of months at Fort Dix were surreal and tough. It felt like being a character in a bad movie that wouldn't end. That complete loser role was mine. If you're tough, prison humbles you; if you're soft, it hardens you. After a few months, I concluded that the federal prison system was broken and a waste of my time. It didn't take long to see that keeping my emotions and mind in check was key to survival. I refused to think negatively, pity myself, or focus on how long my sentence was.

Instead, I chose to take it one week at a time. It didn't take long to realize that establishing a routine to pass the time was essential. Without something to do, I would dwell on my family, which wasn't good for my mental health. The emptiness inside me was a constant feeling. The hole in my life caused by the absence of my family, especially Annie, was unquenchable. I fought against the thoughts in my mind that focused on how much I hurt her, and I was determined not to let these thoughts consume me. More than anything, I didn't want my experience in the criminal justice system to destroy me or my wife, hoping to become someone my wife and family would recognize after this turmoil. There were times when Annie was the strongest among us. She helped me navigate the pain of losing my freedom. Prison is not a good place to be for a long time; it wears you down. With my wife's support, I kept looking forward instead of backward.

  Breakfast was served at 6 am, lunch at 11 am, and dinner at 4 pm We would line up outside the cafeteria, which also served as the TV and game room after dinner. The food was okay, or maybe I just got used to it. There was a small workout room for exercise, or we could go outside to the recreational area when it was open. When the weather permitted, being outside was the best option. The workout room was dingy, with old, often broken equipment. It wasn't uncommon for bloody arguments to occur there. Outside, there was a dirt track, a softball field, basketball, handball, and bocce courts. I even tried yoga, but I didn't find it relaxing, contrary to what people say. Without a doubt, the highlight of my days was seeing my family, but a profound emptiness always followed the visits.

  The visiting area was a small room with a front desk and bench seating. Inmates had to sit across from their visitors, but sometimes we were allowed to hold a small child or hold hands with a loved one. There were two bathrooms: one for inmates and another for their visitors. Visitors were not permitted to bring outside food or other items, but they could purchase snacks, microwaveable meals, and drinks from a vending machine inside the visiting area. Everyone had to follow the rules; if anyone broke them, we would all face consequences. Fortunately, this didn't happen often. Families of different inmates would see each other frequently and get to know one another. Annie's facial expression conveyed her concerns and worries. Did others notice it too, or were they too wrapped up in their own issues? There were times when an illness like chickenpox broke that cause the room to be closed so it could be used to quarantine the sick.

  Every time I saw my wife, I searched her eyes for the love I prayed she still had for me. Over time, I wondered if my visits were too much for her. Seeing her in such a state was a stark reminder of what was left behind at home and how easily we take our freedom for granted. In a way, we were both in prison—

mine being physical and Annie's emotional. My situation affected my entire family. They rearranged their schedules to show me their support.

When something is new, even if it's bad, you try to make the best of it; at least, that was my thinking. There were times when it reached 100 degrees outside, and the building with no air conditioning became an oven. On those days, the thought of not making it to the next day was common.

I made friends, and before long, I became a sort of peacemaker among the inmates. They viewed me as a reasonable person who could diffuse tense situations. This earned me a great deal of respect. Little did I know, this reached the prison warden, which resulted in me gaining esteem. One day, the warden offered me a job I couldn't refuse. He asked if I wanted to be a Town Driver. The position provided an experience that few inmates would ever encounter. Town Drivers can leave the Camp to transport newly released inmates. The idea of this delighted me. I would have never imagined that an incarcerated person could be entrusted with such a task, but that was the case. Of course, safeguards would be in place. The job entailed driving to and from drop-off points without direct supervision. Most importantly, this would be something to do to help pass the time. I accepted the job with a smile and a thank you.

At first, for no clear reason, maybe just another way to pass the time, I started journaling my interactions with some of my passenger inmates, capturing the stories they shared as best I could, hoping that one day, their stories might help someone avoid similar situations.

You Can't Always Go Back –

November 23, 2017

Thanksgiving Eve

In prison, there are a few days you look forward to; one of them is tomorrow, Thanksgiving. You get a special turkey meal, stuffing, corn, mashed potatoes, and a Table Talk pie. The guys trade the pies in hopes of getting a flavor they like. The only drawback is that you eat at 11 am.

I was ready to head to the garage to start my Wednesday. There were a couple of guys going home. One guy was scheduled to get picked up by his family. One released inmate needed to catch a flight. I pulled up to the gate to get my *commuter*. Everything was moving in slow motion. A lot of COs were off for the long weekend. I saw a young man being escorted my way. I sat up straight in the minivan as they approached. The inmate looked to be about 30 years old. He was well-dressed. Most men leave the prison wearing gray sweatpants and a white T-shirt. His garb stood out.

The guy, Luis, got in the vehicle. He needed to be dropped off at the airport in Philly. That drive would take me an hour on a normal day, but because of the Thanksgiving holiday, it might take longer. Luis looked nervous as we pulled away from the prison. I asked him if he was okay.

He said, "I'm afraid of going home."

Luis told me that he lived in La Perla, which has the highest crime rate in Puerto Rico.

"La Perla is loaded with drugs, gangs, and kidnappings," Luis said, "I'm going to a halfway house, and fear I'll be gunned down once I get there."

He explained that he had been involved in transporting firearms from Florida to Puerto Rico. Tampa was the home base for a major drug ring, and there was a significant bust there in late 2009. He was a part of it.

"My role was to purchase firearms from licensed dealers and sell the guns to convicted felons. The dealers winked at what was happening. Greed is a strong impulse, moving them to make the sales anyway. The weapons were then used to commit violent crimes, mostly drug-related, throughout Puerto Rico."

Luis said the FBI arrested many police officers on the island who were helping the drug gangs. Luis started sweating as we approached the airport. He asked me what he should do. I told him what came to mind.

"Go home and start a new life."

I could feel him looking at me. It seemed that he wanted more advice.

He said, "That is impossible. When I got arrested, I provided the DEA and FBI with information about the gun ring."

Because Luis cooperated by giving information to the law enforcement agencies, he only served seven years in prison. Most of his time, he said, was spent at Fort Dix. Luis said that he expected help from the gang when he got arrested. He didn't say it, but I suspected many guys were arrested based on Luis' information. He confirmed that his family had to flee Puerto Rico because gang members threatened to kill them.

Drugs, gangs, and guns are all things we read about or see on TV, but Luis was someone who lived that life. He was 16 years old when he joined a gang. How does someone escape from a past like that?

Luis's comments were believable when he said he would likely be killed when he reached Puerto Rico. He told me that the police could not help because some of the police officers were involved in the drug ring, and they, too, had been arrested. He could not trust the officers who remained. Talking to Luis made me think about questions I had not considered, like who do you trust if you can't trust the police? I asked Luis if he had told anyone at Fort Dix, a CO or counselor, about his fear of returning home.

"What would be the point? Those *expletives deleted* lazy excuses for humans didn't care. They didn't want to get involved in any way."

One of the many quirks released inmates face is that they are required to return to their previous city of residence. There is no consideration for circumstances, such as the risk of being targeted and killed by returning to the 'scene of the crime.' I suspect the idea is to get those being released back to the city, where their family lived. The major flaw in this logic is that, in many cases, a divorce breaks up the family, and the spouse who is left behind moves away. The BOP goes by another name inside: Backward On Purpose. After reading the accounts in this book, you may agree the name is appropriate and well earned.

When we arrived at the airport, it was busy with holiday travelers. Luis's stop was JetBlue Airlines. I put the vehicle in park and gave Luis his boarding instructions. He nodded. As Luis exited the vehicle, I wished him well and drove off. I looked forward to the turkey and fixings that were coming the next day.

Back at the garage, it was almost time for everyone to return and close for the evening. The inmates working in the garage loaded into the minivan, and we returned to Camp. We had dinner at 4 pm. After a count at 9:30 pm, we had another count at 10 pm. I got a call to go to the CO's office. I was tired, but not worried. The CO on duty was nice. Upon reaching the office, the CO said,

"Finazzo, the guy you dropped off today at the airport, what was he wearing?"

Thinking about it for a minute, I told him what I could remember.

"A dark pair of jeans and a black Nike hoodie. Why?"

The CO said Luis never boarded his flight to Puerto Rico. He said the airport video showed me dropping him off, but Luis never got on the plane. Based on what Luis had shared, I was not surprised. I was allowed to return to my bunk and thought about Thanksgiving, grateful I could sleep until 7 am.

The CO called me back to the office in the afternoon on Thanksgiving Day. A different officer was on duty. "Finazzo, your passenger, Luis, was picked up a few hours earlier by the US Marshal Service. He had purchased another ticket and boarded a plane to Miami.

He was arrested a few minutes before takeoff. He's ended his chance for freedom."

I wondered how Luis would spend his Thanksgiving and what would happen to him next.

Chapter 12 – Reaching For Some Control – January 2017

I was managing my life at Fort Dix. Some days were better than others, but I was managing. My family visited often, and I had made some friends while working as a town driver. Winter was in full swing, which made life at Fort Dix more difficult. This may be due to the anticipation of numerous family holiday gatherings that with carry on without me.

    I woke up at 5 am to shower, eager to start the day. It had snowed overnight, so the vehicles needed clearing. I took the keys from the officer on duty and tried to hide my annoyance when he asked for my ID. Even though my face was familiar, the rules were the rules, and following them was the smart move. Not wanting to do anything that might risk my opportunity, since being able to drive gave me a much-needed sense of normalcy. Although the job wasn't always easy, with the constant pressure from the guys to smuggle things for them, it made me feel useful. I often thought my punishment didn't match my *crime,* whatever that might be. The decision wasn't mine; community service seemed more fitting, or doing something to help the less fortunate would have made more sense. Someone told me that God put me in prison to help people who could benefit from my work experiences. This never made much sense, since my time at Fort Dix felt like a waste. I could have contributed to society instead of just being a ward. That all changed during one of my transport trips.

Inspiration - January 2017

Six guys were heading to two separate locations. Three were going to the Philadelphia airport, and three to the Philly bus station on Filbert Street. The list of people leaving had been given to me, and my route was planned. The stop was on the East Side of the complex, then I would take the half-mile drive to the other side. After loading the van with my new group, the airport would be the first drop-off point.

Some guys were coming out as I pulled up to my designated pick-up spot. Several wore clothing sent from home, while others wore gray sweats bought at the commissary. In federal prisons, inmates cannot wear certain colors. Anything other than white, gray, or brown is forbidden. The inmates in the low ward wear a brown uniform, unlike the green worn in Camp.

    I asked for each person's name before letting anyone into the vehicle. Once they loaded up, we headed out. From the chatter, it was clear that the guys were excited to be going home. The remaining men waited outside as the van pulled into the West Side parking area. After verifying their names, the men got into the van, and we headed for the exit gate. The men started talking about the next chapter of their lives, sharing their thoughts on what each would do when he got home. I listened while driving, interested to hear if the prison had served them well. As they spoke, it occurred to me that most of the guys had no training or experience for the jobs they wanted to pursue. Most had been in and out of the system for years; some had never held a legitimate job. Someone mentioned wanting to start a clothing line, which made my ears perk up. Another guy said he wanted to buy and sell real estate. They were discussing running businesses, but they lacked the basic knowledge or skills to make those businesses successful.

One of the men said, "Man, I wish there was some training that they could give us in prison so when we get out, we can run a legal business. You know, do it right."

His comment made me think about how I could help the guys in the Camp prepare for the lives they wanted to lead outside. This trip represented a pivotal moment for me. During the first six months of my sentence, my only focus was on myself, wondering if I would be okay and safe. Never having been in trouble before, this BOP situation was new to the BOP and to this way of life. Leaving my family behind was difficult. Every step it took to walk into the prison lobby to check myself in and begin my sentence was engraved as if a book was planted in my head. It didn't matter that I believed in my innocence; the details of what had occurred were irrelevant.

There was no special treatment for being successful before coming to prison. It didn't matter how much money anyone once had. I was a convicted felon, living among other convicted felons. Rich, poor, black, or white, we were all assigned prison numbers. Who was *good*? Who was *bad*? Innocent or guilty, who cared? We were all in the same place. Some of us would eventually return home to pick up the pieces, with our education, family, and money to help ease the transition. Others, like the guys in the van on this day, would struggle to find their way. The system had failed these men.

    After sixty minutes, we reached the airport. The first group stepped out. None of them had ever been on a plane, so they were unsure what to do. I gave them instructions and grabbed their garbage bags, also known as prison luggage. After shaking their hands, we said goodbye. Although I would never see them again, my sincere hope was that they would find support and success and avoid returning to prison. The idea of guys spending their lives in and out of prison didn't sit well with me. My thoughts shifted to how I could help make a difference.

Chapter 13 – Giving Back – May 2017

Permission to teach had been granted. Interestingly, aside from some basic questions like the course titles and brief descriptions, no guidelines were provided. Since the class times were after dinner, the sole 'education staff' would be gone when the material was presented to the class. The CO on duty was content to stay in his tiny space, so classes were taught without supervision.

    Annie could see my excitement when I told her. She was happy for me, as if a dim light had reignited. When she asked if there was anything she could do to help, I already had something in mind: getting my lesson plans typed. She said she would make sure that happened. That was the clinching factor for this to move forward. I took my time and thought about what would be most helpful. Starting with the basics seemed appropriate, while being careful not to insult the students. The idea was to share useful information—things they would encounter in any normal business class. I considered how to present the information, wanting to include relatable examples and topics they would be interested in pursuing.

The materials for each course were about thirty pages, handwritten on notepaper. Once I was satisfied with each handout, they were sent home to be typed. There was a copier in the classroom. I requested copies, and an inmate with access to the machine made them. A copy was printed for each inmate who signed up. My favorite course was Concept to Profit, and the men loved it. Each course was extended to thirteen weeks to align with the schedule and avoid being too rigorous. The length also helped the men grasp traditional business concepts. To my delight, many of them gained real insights into running a business, and they made solid plans to start their own upon release. They understood the importance of having a business plan, doing market research, and considering contingencies. Teaching and working as a Town Driver made for some "good" days. Still, I never forgot my unpleasant accommodations.

Good days aside, being in prison was not easy. It's crucial to stay alert at all times. Being aware of what was happening around me was essential. There was always something going on. Being well-liked helped keep me safe. When trouble was about to happen, like a group of men targeting someone or attacking a *troublemaker*, I received a warning to stay away from the area where the *action* would take place. If an attack was going to happen near my bunk, I was told to stay in the recreation room until a certain time to avoid getting caught in the crossfire. On those nights, it was harder than usual to fall asleep. The morning after these incidents reminded me how lucky I was to have friends who looked out for me and did the same for them. *Connections* in prison are priceless because it's a place that can make you feel isolated.

I was certain that the hands on every clock in prison had arthritis because time passed so slowly. Having things to do, like my family's visits, teaching inmates how to be entrepreneurs, working, and forming genuine friendships with other inmates, helped me maintain my sanity.

There was nothing extraordinary about my day-to-day life. Like many other inmates, I was simply serving my time. Along the way, many lessons were learned about life, people, the prison structure, and myself. Making a few good friends was important, none more special than Dan. I would have never guessed that the first guy who approached me arrival at Fort Dix would come to mean so much to me. He left Fort Dix after serving 38 months. When Dan left, I discovered the first of two ways to track time in prison, neither of which involved using a calendar. The first way to track time was through friendships. When you meet people in prison, one of the most common questions is, "How much time do you have?" or "How much time do you have left?" You unconsciously commit to memory the release dates of your friends. When they leave, you know how much time has passed. The second way to track time was not learned until much later.

They Called Him Biggs – September 2017

Pizza night is where friendships are made. It's one of the closest things to *family time* you'll experience in prison. We buy what we need from the commissary to make pizza and strombolis. We start the preparation at our bunks and then use the microwave in the kitchen to cook them for three minutes.

We were cooking the pizzas when an announcement over the speaker called for me to come to the officer's station for an immediate release. As fast as possible, I got into my uniform, put on my boots, picked up the phone and keys from the officers' station, and headed toward the van. When I reached the East Side, a CO and the released inmate were waiting for me. The CO instructed me to take the guy to the Philly bus station, letting me know he needed to catch a 10 pm bus to North Carolina. The man was very large, older, and carrying his luggage: three full garbage bags. As was my routine, the bags were placed in the back, and I asked my passenger if he wanted to ride in the backseat or the front. He opted for the backseat. Once we were on our way, we engaged in small talk. He told me to call him "Biggs." To start the trip, I asked Biggs about his crime.

"I managed money for seniors. They trusted me, which made it easy to swindle them. I told them I was investing their Social Security payments, but used their money to enjoy a lavish lifestyle. I created false financial reports to prove my brilliant investment strategy. In total, I stole more than $8 million."

Although Biggs said he regretted his actions, I didn't believe him.

While driving, Biggs began to breathe hard and hold his chest. He started to hyperventilate. This wasn't surprising; I had seen quite a few guys get nervous on their way home. I took out a small plastic bag and gave it to him, explaining that I couldn't stop; he would have to deal with his situation on his own. My responsibility was to get him to the bus station and try to be at the Camp in time for the count. Calling was an option if I couldn't make it, but that was frowned upon; the COs did not like to do a ghost count.

Once Biggs caught his breath, he told me that he was arrested by the FBI and IRS agents at his home.

"They were at my front door at 5 am. They lined up my wife, my kids, and me against the wall. I was arrested on the spot and taken into custody. I haven't been home since."

Biggs said his wife divorced him after his arrest, and she and the kids moved out of the state. He mentioned that it was nine years ago. He said he was lucky that a judge reduced his 14-year sentence to time served, since he had been given extra time for preying on the elderly.

Listening to Biggs made me remember when the FBI showed up at my house and arrested me in front of Annie and Shanna. Biggs lost everything—his family, friends, and lifestyle. As we pulled up to the bus station to let Biggs out, I thought about my family. I couldn't wait to get back to them, but for the moment, my focus was to rush back to the Camp for the count and, hopefully, some leftover pizza.

Chapter 14 – A Helping Hand – January 2018

I taught classes and worked as a town driver for five years. Through my classes, over 300 men learned about how things work in an honest business. Some of them sent me letters expressing their gratitude for my efforts, and many wished they could have received the information in their younger years because it might have kept them out of prison. I will never be proud of how circumstances at work led me to a situation where Fort Dix became part of my story. I will always take pride in my efforts to help the men there.

January 2018

To Chris Finazzo:

Chris, thank you so much for your time and effort that you dedicate to all of us, teaching us how to better our lives and not come back to prison.
Your classrooms have been very inspiring and helpful, and have given me the opportunity to better

myself and prepare myself to become a better person and a role model to my family once I am released from here.

I enjoy being around you and learning as much as I can. I'm thankful for you spending time with me and walking me through the process of retail and what it takes to be a CEO of a public company. Also, answering all my questions that needed to be answered.

You have become a mentor to me and the older brother I never had. Again, thanks for everything. Get home to your family. I hope to see you again soon.

    Your friend,
    Alex B.

My granddaughter Valentina was seven years old when I went to prison. I missed all the birthdays that led up to her becoming a teenager and the births of six new grandchildren. Life at home went on without me, which made me sad and, at the same time, glad—happy that they were carrying on, trying to live as normal a life as possible. They never stopped visiting me, but my yearning to be home with them was a constant in my mind. Home was my dream, the place I felt I belonged. Getting out of this mess of a place was my biggest goal. Having limited and supervised visits with my family was frustrating. Holding onto hope kept me grounded. I decided to try to get back to them sooner than my sentence allowed. I had served three-quarters of my time and believed that should be enough. I had been a model inmate, never causing trouble. It was time for me to go home. Of course, it wasn't my decision, but I felt like one of Santa's elves watching children open their presents. That's when I started to reconnect with my faith, which I had strayed from early in adulthood due to work and time. Growing up in the church and believing in God had been the foundation of my life. I only hoped that He remembered me. I needed Him to bring me home as soon as possible. That was my prayer.

My prayer was answered in an unexpected way. Although keeping up with politics wasn't a top priority, I was serving alongside senators and other congressional representatives who remained well-informed about Washington, DC. They had read about pending legislation, policy changes, and everything related to pardons and sentence commutations. Many inmates joked about receiving a "get out of jail free card" from the President, but the former political officials at Fort Dix had insight into an upcoming bill. If passed by Congress, the bill would significantly impact federal prison reform.

A law called the First Step Act was being given serious considered. If it became law, federal prisons would assess prisoners' risk of reoffending and decide who could be released early. I saw this as an opportunity I couldn't ignore. I listened, learned, and waited. Finally, the news came that President Trump signed the bill into law in December 2018. Ultimately, through a First Step Act program, I was approved for early release after serving five and a half years of my eight-year sentence. I was excited about going home early to my family. At last, I'd be a passenger instead of the town driver.

When a person is leaving prison to go home, their mindset shifts; they no longer want to think about how they ended up there. No more wondering, wasted time, or idle dreaming. Now, there is a real date to get out. If you have boots, you give them away; shorts, T-shirts, and food all go to guys who can't afford anything. You choose the guys who need it most. Guys in prison struggle without support from family and friends. When you work, you get paid 30 to 40 cents an hour. If your family can't help, you're on your own. My focus shifted to improving my physical and mental health. I also started giving away things that were no longer needed. With fewer friends than when I arrived, as many had finished their sentences. The items went to those who were still stuck in the rodent trap, those who needed things the most. I gave away clothing, food, and essential hygiene items, like *toilet paper* and laundry detergent. It was exciting thinking about not being subjected to headcounts, midnight raids, and snoring bunkmates for much longer.

According to the news, the country had panicked over COVID-19. The disease was labeled a pandemic, but we didn't give it the same attention inside the prison. We didn't have the physical space to maintain six feet apart. The prison administration implemented a new rule to ensure that no inmate leaving Fort Dix would spread the virus. They mandated that every prisoner scheduled for release had to spend 15 days in isolation. I was informed my treasured date would be April 15, 2020. I thought to myself that God surely had a sense of humor; my exit from prison was going to be just as traumatic as my entrance, and a return to the SHU would have to be endured again.

I told my bunkmate, James, about the new isolation rule, and he chuckled. James hated the SHU more than most people. He was a good guy, but he had one bad day. His wife used to visit him every week with their son, consistently for two years. One day, James received a letter from her saying she didn't want to be with him anymore. The news devastated him, and he lashed out, landing himself in the SHU. While in the SHU, he experienced a full-blown panic attack. That's why he hated it. When he told me what happened, I asked how he managed. That's when I learned about the second way to keep track of time.

James told me he was given toilet paper and a blanket in the SHU. He said he broke off one piece of toilet paper daily to track the days until he was released into the general population. He mentioned that this act helped him remember that an end was in sight. On April 1st, I broke off my first piece of toilet paper in the SHU. That night, my thoughts drifted to what I had endured and why I was there. Of course, this made me think about my former friend and boss. To my surprise, I no longer harbored contempt for him; he was simply someone who was once a friend. Like all friendships, we had times when we didn't get along. He was a complicated guy with a lot of issues.

Nonetheless, he had built something that few people could have accomplished. I would always respect him for that. I didn't want to kill or praise him, nor judge him. If prison, specifically being a Town Driver, had taught me anything, it was not to judge.

Alone in the SHU, I prayed every day and night until I had broken off 15 squares of toilet paper and could go home.

The Last Dance - March 2020

It's late March 2020, and it's time for me to go home. My sentence was cut short by eighteen months because of the First Step Act. Sometimes, you get lucky, and things go your way.

The world was changing as COVID-19 affected every city in America. One of the advantages of being a Town Driver is that you get to see what is happening in the outside world each day. The guards at the gate were now wearing masks and checking every car that arrived. I still hadn't been given a mask, and the changes in the outside world and at the Camp made me wonder what was going on. A common cold in prison is a reason for concern. My departure date is sixteen days away, and I want to do everything possible to make sure that nothing goes wrong during these final days. It was a chilly day in late March. The frosty air made me shiver.

Reflections Of A Town Driver

I was wondering how this COVID-19 virus would affect my release date. It's a prison, so anything is possible. People are dying; the challenges cities and their people were having were constant messages on the radio. Concern about my health and my ability to go home dominated my thoughts.

Two guys on the West Side are getting out today. Both came out on time, and the guards wore masks and told me to stay in the van. That was unusual. I have been doing this for five years; this has never happened before. The guys climb into the van and confirm they are going to the Philly bus and the Philly Halfway House. That's near the children's hospital in North Philly.

It would take me a few hours to make the trip. My first stop is the Philly bus station. Everyone is wearing a mask. Why, I asked myself, is it that bad? There is little conversation with the passengers other than about what is happening worldwide. At the first drop-off, I realized this could be my last trip. The outside world looks like something out of a horror movie. Few people are on the street, and those out are wearing masks and walking fast without acknowledging others passing by.

My last passenger, Ralph, is an older white man in his 60s. We're about thirty-five minutes from the halfway house, and Ralph shares a wild story with me.

"My wife passed away about five years ago from cancer. I was devastated. I couldn't even attend her funeral, man, how nasty is that? Showing my pain in that place would have been a mistake. You know, most of the guys would have shown no mercy.

"I owned a successful business in Philly, and my sons worked in the business too. I would see their trucks on the road every day."

I listened to him with skepticism. He told me he needed someone to clean his house because his wife was ill and in a nursing home. He was recommended to a service that would do that, so he called the service and got someone to clean for him.

"The first lady was in her mid-50s. She cleans the house every week. She did a great job."

What he tells me next is hard to believe.

"The older woman was replaced with a much younger girl. I wasn't sure how old she was."

He attempted to explain that he had been deceived, yet the expression on his face conveyed something different.

"She would clean my house and stay to make dinner; she did other things besides her cleaning chores. *Ya* know, extra stuff. She was with me for three months."

You hear stories like this, but I never thought they were real.

"One day, she called and said that she was not coming over any longer unless I paid her $5,000. I was *kinda* stunned. So, I asked why, and she told me she was under 18, and the agency would make my life difficult if I didn't pay. I gave her the *f...ing* $5,000, but they keep asking for more. One day, I didn't pay, and found myself handcuffed by the FBI for child prostitution."

Ralph is caught up in a prostitution ring. He tells me his family will meet him at the halfway house. I know if that happens to a family member, few families show up to welcome him back. As I pull up to the gate, a group of people is waiting for Ralph; his family has come to welcome him home. Seeing his family, I'm inclined to believe his narrative. Wishing him well as he exits the van, my next stop would be the Camp.

Driving through the streets, the seriousness of this COVID situation is clear. The streets show how serious this virus is. Only a few people are outside, and those who are wear masks. As I pass City Hall, I see many EMTs and police officers outside. When I reach the prison gate, things have changed in the last four hours. Guards are wearing hazmat suits; the scene looks like something from a horror movie. I'm told to see the Camp director. *What's going on?*

In a gruff, unwelcoming voice, the Director states, "Finazzo, you're going home on the fifteenth of April 2020. You will be staying in the SHU for your remaining time here. If you refuse, you will not be going home."

He finishes with a dismissive glare. No one should have to spend any time in the SHU; it is a bad place. Food is delivered through a vent in the door, and the lights turn on at 5 am and off at 11 pm Some guys spend years in the SHU. You sometimes end up in a cell with another inmate.

    This time, I would be staying with another inmate. The two of us made the best of it for fourteen days. This was my final indignity before being released. My fate was sealed for *my protection* to keep me away from the population; it was intended to isolate me from COVID. Some of the *amenities* of being in the SHU include being handcuffed while showering in a locked cell. Clean underwear and clothes are given to you every few days. The *guests* bang on the doors and walls at night and never stop screaming. They throw their food out of the door slot, with apples being the favorite to toss. As I wait to go home with COVID-19 spreading, I often wonder how I ended up here and why. I'm here to share my stories so that others won't have to go through this hell the way I did. To all the guys I drove home—hundreds of them—I hope you find peace in your lives.

Chapter 15 – The Lights Are Back On – April 2020

After my time at Fort Dix, I slowly eased back into civilian life. I'm sure I drove Annie, my kids, and the rest of my family crazy because of my constant need to be around them. While they couldn't understand it, their physical presence made me feel better. Being back at home was wonderful for many reasons, but it came with issues I didn't dare share with them. I refused to burden anyone with my problems. Despite my efforts, the smallest things would trigger overreactions, like a knock at the door or walking down the basement stairs. I would be having a casual conversation with Annie, and out of nowhere, an image of her crying in the middle of our living room would flash through my mind.

    Sleeping was the most difficult task. This was ironic because it was the one thing I most looked forward to doing when I was away. Although I was in the home, I cherished, next to the woman I loved, sleep evaded me. Every stir of the wind, every passing car on our street, and the creaks of our house made me think I was back at the Camp. My mind would not rest, with constant thoughts about what happened to me running through my head. My life had been taken away from me, and even though I was released from Fort Dix, I was struggling to reclaim it. I struggled to see myself as the man I once was. I hid my feelings and put a smile on my face for my family's sake, expecting the difficulties to pass, and I would feel like *myself* again.

    As time went on, I started to see a few people outside of my family, mainly neighbors and longtime friends, with whom Annie and I shared. Whenever I met them, we never discussed my time at Fort Dix. I was glad not to bring it up, but the bracelet on my ankle served as a constant reminder. Wearing it was part of my probation, along with the requirement to call in weekly to my probation officer and get permission before traveling out of state. The latter was the most inconvenient, but necessary to keep my freedom, so I followed the rules.

    Annie had retired and loved being an active grandmother. I also enjoyed spending time with the grandkids; each of them was a blessing. I missed Valentina's sweet giggle.

How much wasn't clear to me until this moment. She had grown into quite a softball player. I attended as many of her practices and games as possible, but I still wasn't ready for full-time grandpa duty. I considered myself too young to retire and too old to work too hard.

Through a personal connection, I secured a position as Director of New Business Development at a construction company. It didn't matter whether they needed my help; I was happy they wanted me there and confident in my ability to add value to the team.

Annie reminded me every day that she loved me. She became stronger over the years of my incarceration. It was easy to see. The way she carried herself was self-confident. She held her head high and carried a smile as if to wipe away tears. I was thankful that she never took me up on the many times I asked her to divorce me. As she did for all those miserable years, Annie encouraged me to look ahead. Whenever I looked into her eyes, my heart told me that we, as a family, would be okay.

Life was good, and I expected that it would only get better.

A Movie Plot - January 2020

I wasn't feeling well last night; there had been a lot of activity in the dorm, including a raid at midnight. This is a procedure used by the prison when it suspects something is going on. They shake down lockers and look for drugs, alcohol, contraband, and food taken from the kitchen. Yes, guys take food out of the kitchen and sell it for stamps, the prison currency. While a shake down is underway, inmates stand beside their lockers as corrections officers and management dig through your property, throwing things out on the floor or bunk. Sometimes, they find nothing as they did tonight. It's not an easy thing to sleep in a dorm with 400 men. Tonight, I knew getting sleep would be difficult. After the 5:00 am count, I showered and prepared for another day. It was very cold, and for some reason, I didn't feel like driving today. That was very rare. I can't remember a day when that was the case. I got in the van and drove to the garage, where the CO in charge gave me my day's work.

"Finazzo, you got 12 guys today, Philly bus. Philly Air, Philly Halfway house, and Newark Airport."

That's a lot of guys to drive in one day, especially in the cold with snow in the forecast. This was the largest number of inmates I've had to transport in a single day. The van seemed ready for the day's travels. I ensured the mechanics in the garage gave it a thorough check and requested new windshield wipers. The crew in the garage were great. They conducted a complete check. Most of them are eager to do anything that makes the day go by faster.

My first stop was picking up ten guys on the West Side; the second was on the East Side. I have to get 12 guys to their locations from 8 am to 3 pm, almost impossible. But as my passengers get in and get settled, they all ask me if they can be first. I have a schedule to follow that maps the shortest amount of time between stops. Seven guys are going to Philly to catch a bus. Everyone is excited to be going home or to a halfway house.

One guy looks lost. I asked him for his paperwork, and he told me he was going to the Philly airport, but he had a ticket for Newark. I asked his name. He told me his name was

Reflections Of A Town Driver 174

Ralph. As I pulled up to the bus station, the guys got out of the van with their stuff. Seven guys getting out at one place is easy to handle. Everyone is eager to get on with their lives. I return to the van, drive a block, and do a headcount. I should have five guys left. I have four. Who is missing? It's Ralph. The Philly bus is not an airport. I back up a block, and Ralph is standing outside the bus station. I asked him, "What the F— are you doing?"

He says, "I thought this was Newark."

"Get in the van. I told you you're the last stop. Why did you get out?"

"I'm nervous, man. This is a big deal."

I can understand that; I did not have a chance to ask him why. I planned on asking once we were alone.

I dropped off the four other guys. It's now past noon. The challenge now was to get Ralph to Newark airport and back within 3 hours. I ask Ralph to jump in the front seat. We are one hour and ten minutes away. "Where are you from, Ralph?"

"Abilene, Texas. I've been in prison for fifteen years. I'm worried about how I'm going to get along. I was a federal employee and supervisor at a post office in the town; I couldn't live on my salary."

"Why were you unable to make ends meet on your salary?"

"Because I had two families."

"What do you mean by two families?"

I was shocked. Two families. I looked at him. He is about 45 years old and has been serving a fifteen-year sentence. I thought *this seemed like something out of a Hollywood movie plot.*

He answered. "I ran a scam where I refunded stamps that were never purchased. Since I was in charge, I got away with it. I sold the stamps at a discount to people outside of my area. I got away
with it for a long time until an internal audit. This was my big mistake that cost me everything."

"What about the two families? How did that happen?"

I was going fast on the NJ Turnpike. Ralph looked at me and said,

"I was married to a wonderful woman who managed a
Supermarket. We have one son. Things were great until I met

another woman and had a daughter with her. I never told my wife, but I always wanted to."

At this point, I told him I was sorry to hear all this. He had made lots of bad decisions. He, like many men, had nowhere to go. His son is now 20, and he has not seen him for 15 years. His daughter is eighteen, and she doesn't remember him. He puts his hands to his face and cries out loud to the Lord to help him find his way. It's hard to watch a man cry real tears. Ralph has suffered enough from his own mistakes. The E-ZPass toll is coming up. We're five minutes from Newark airport. I told Ralph to get himself together.

"You will be fine. Try and reconnect with your kids."

His wife, the mother of his daughter, had remarried, and he said that they live in different states. He will live with his brother, who is 20 years older than him, and try to restart his life.

We pulled up to the terminal and wished him well. He starts to cry as he exits the van. As I pull away, I wonder how things happen to people

and why. Ralph was a poor decision-maker,
but he put in his time
and should have a chance for a fresh start.

    The end of a long day, and I'm more
excited to go home to my family with each
passing hour. I pulled into the gate at 2:55.
My thoughts were to get a good night's sleep
and dream of home.

Chapter 16 – Closing The Door - November 2022

I had been home for almost three years, living happily and free. Since leaving Fort Dix, I hadn't revisited the inmate stories captured as a Town Driver. One ending was missing, but I couldn't write it because I disliked it. Today, that has changed.

My name is Chris Finazzo. I served over five-and-a-half years at Fort Dix Federal Correctional Institution and have always believed in my innocence. Today, I received a message from my friend and attorney, Alan Lewis, at Carter Ledyard & Milburn, the law firm that represented me during my trial. Alan had left a message indicating that a turn of events relevant to my case had occurred. In his message, he asked me to see him as soon as possible. His actual words were, "I have good news."

I had put my case and my time at Fort Dix behind me. And had no desire to reopen old wounds for myself or my family.

I talked to Annie about the message and his request to meet with him. We decided to accept the meeting, but we agreed not to tell our children anything. A few days later, the meeting was scheduled. The law firm had relocated, so I requested the new address. Upon arrival at the office, I was unprepared for the information being shared.

    I listened carefully to Alan's words, trying to understand everything. Alan was part of a team of attorneys on my case. When the lead attorney retired, Alan's interest never waned. He decided to follow a similar case, the Ciminelli case, in the Supreme Court. His perspective focused on how it could apply to me. He reached out when his intuition sensed that the Supreme Court would likely reject the Right To Control argument. Alan had participated in representing me at the trial and during my appeal with the Second Circuit. I was grateful that he took the time to follow the case to its conclusion. He maintained a constant interest in my case over the years because he always felt that I had suffered an unjust conviction and sentence. It takes dedication to stand up for the rights of a defendant whom an attorney believes has been mistreated.

Unsure if I understood what Alan had said. I reminded him that the Second Circuit Court had denied my request for an appeal.

He said, "I know; that's my point."

My head was spinning. I felt light-headed and must have turned pale.

Struggling to understand what Alan said, I held my breath, hoping a path to redemption was unfolding. Would the Supreme Court intervene in a way that would benefit me? Still confused, I resisted getting my hopes up to avoid being disappointed once again.

Shaking off my confusion, I asked, "The Supreme Court?"

He confirmed, "Yes, the United States Supreme Court." He added, "Not only did they hear the argument last fall, but they have released an opinion on the matter."

> Justice Thomas delivered the opinion of the Court on May 11, 2023. It stated, "In this case, we must decide whether the Second Circuit's longstanding 'right to control' theory of fraud describes a valid basis for liability under the federal wire fraud statute…under the right-to-control

theory, a defendant is guilty of wire fraud if he schemes to deprive the victim of 'potentially valuable economic information' 'necessary to make discretionary economic decisions.'...the federal fraud statutes criminalize only schemes to deprive people of traditional property interests...because 'potentially valuable economic information' 'necessary to make discretionary economic decisions' is not a traditional property interest, we now hold that the right-to-control theory is not a valid basis for liability....the right-to-control theory is invalid under the federal fraud statutes. We, therefore, reverse the judgment of the Court of Appeals and remand the case for further proceedings consistent with this opinion. It is so ordered."

Having learned from the politicians I met at Fort Dix that the Supreme Court's opinion papers reveal the justices' leanings regarding their rulings. The justices were unanimous in their opinions. Was he saying what I thought he was saying?

I can't state it verbatim, but my takeaway from the meeting was that all signs indicated the Supreme Court would rule the mail wire fraud charges of which I was found guilty had a strong chance of being vacated. In the end, due to my fraud convictions being vacated, this entire nightmare ended with a sole conviction under the Travel Act. This resulted in a conviction for committing a New York misdemeanor and for theoretically agreeing to commit an act of fraud that was never actually carried out.

In conclusion, the vacated fraud convictions left behind a thought crime (conspiracy) and a federalized misdemeanor. I served years in prison for a putative *crime* that was not a crime.

Alan and his team attempted to recover the restitution money the government had taken, but once it's gone, it's gone. I theoretically still owed 18 million dollars to the government. While it's hard to believe, all of the debt was canceled through the efforts of my lawyers in getting my right to control convictions overturned. As we sometimes read, ADAs in the Department of Justice can be overzealous. Like most people, they want to win. In this case, their victory came at my great expense. The case should never have been prosecuted. For me, I'm happy with the final result, my *redemption.* Now I can continue my life with the burden of a huge lien removed and my name cleared. I can't change the past. I can live my life knowing my ethics have not faltered. I had been true to my employer and, most important, to myself.

You often hear that lawyers aren't any good; however, that was not the case with Alan Lewis. I'm so grateful for all the work he did to follow my case and for helping me become a whole person again.

The Supreme Court will officially rule in less than sixty days. Would Annie notice a missing roll of toilet paper?

I'm now free, and my reputation has been restored. However, like many other innocent men and women, *no one can give me back the time lost—time to spend with my family, to see my grandchildren be born and grow, and to share moments with the woman I love.*

I am one of the lucky ones. My family stood by me. I returned to a loving home and am now experiencing the joy of being a grandparent. Lost time can never be recaptured, though I can put it in the past and carry on. Hold my head high and light up with a broad grin when I hear the word *freedom*.

Yes, I am a grateful, lucky man. If you will recall this:

"It is better to let the crime of a guilty person go unpunished than to condemn the innocent." As stated in a 1895 U.S. Supreme Court case.

It is as true today as it was back in the 19th century.

The result of the Supreme Court ruling is that all mail wire fraud counts have been vacated.

Counts 2-16: The right to control is not a crime. To think that I spent all this time and money fighting something I did not do makes me angry. I never understood the right to control charges—something an overzealous DOJ would charge you with that no one understands. I know that the jury of my peers did not understand the crime, but they found me guilty. Nobody once said, "What are the charges in this case?"

Count 1 - Conspiring to violate the Travel Act is the only count not vacated because it is separate from the Supreme Court ruling. The

US Attorney's Office wants to win at all costs, regardless of the defendant. They have more resources and can do whatever they want. The DOJ is a government agency that takes resources from people charged with financial crimes—innocent or not—and seizes what they want. I recall the high-fives in the courtroom when I was found guilty by the DOJ team, as if they had won the Super Bowl, including the US Attorney for the Eastern District. She later became the US Attorney General. It's a big political game played with very high stakes. Any money a defendant had, including that needed for their defense, is confiscated. People's lives are forever changed because the DOJ's DA and ADAs are motivated by their desire to advance politically.

I now understand how the system works and what you need to do to fight for your rights, no matter how hard it may be, at all costs. As of this writing, I have reached an agreement with the DOJ. I am ready to let that go and move on from this.

NEVER GIVE UP HOPE THAT THINGS WILL GET BETTER AND TURN AROUND.

Things have changed for me, though I'm among the few lucky ones.

Afterword

Usually, the individual who pens the foreword or, in this case, the book's Afterword, is well-known—I am not. The tasks of writing these sections and editing a book are distinct roles. I assisted with the writing by posing questions, offering suggestions, and providing initial edits. Everything about the creation of this book is unique, which aligns with what Chris Finazzo shared with me.

My name is Naceema Samira. I am an African American woman and have been self-employed for over twenty years, providing small businesses with project management, strategic planning, and writing and editing services. In a highly social world, I survive by word-of-mouth referrals. For this reason, I wasn't surprised to receive a phone call from an unknown individual who said, "I was told maybe you could help me."

During our first conversation, Chris explained that he knew my brother Robert from working in the fashion industry. He mentioned he was a former executive at a well-known retail chain and that he was charged with a crime he didn't understand was a crime. He was confident in his innocence. Not realizing that an action is a crime is not unusual. Without much consideration, I thought, "Well, that's a terrible defense!"

Chris told me he had journaled his interactions with the men he drove out of Fort Dix, a federal correctional institution. He mentioned wanting to share their stories in a book and described some of his entries to me. I was intrigued, as I was familiar with several people involved in our criminal justice system; however, none of them were middle-aged, professional white men. My family had our house raided because neighbors suspected drug activity was taking place inside, based on nothing more than an incorrect assumption. This, coupled with the political and racial conflicts that permeate our daily news cycle, resulted in me having issues with our legal process. Despite this, I agreed to help, thinking, "This should be interesting!"

Over several months, I participated in phone conversations and emails with this *stranger* to help him bring his vision to light. After several discussions, it became clear that I was interacting with a remarkable storyteller. I sensed that there was much he wasn't

Reflections Of A Town Driver

sharing. I encouraged Chris to open up about his experiences and the stories of the men he encountered. He agreed. I believe the inclusion of his journey makes this book a fascinating read. On the surface, it offers a unique glimpse into prison life, the choices that lead to incarceration, and the impact on inmates' families. That alone is significant. However, this book does something more. It invites the reader to (re)evaluate their views on loyalty, criminality, and empathy without lecturing them. I gave Chris a homework assignment to help him organize his thoughts.

This work proves that Chris was open to challenges. His recounting is filled with incredible situations and surprising outcomes. This book is pure dedication to non-fiction, though it reads like a novel, which I love. Often, my discussions with Chris ended with me shaking my head in disbelief, rolling my eyes in frustration, and smiling hours after our call ended. Chris revealed his heart and his hurt to me. Throughout these pages, he willingly shares the same with you.

I'm thrilled with the way this project turned out and grateful to have been a part of it. This is Chris's story, his truth, and his redemption. I hope you enjoyed the read as much as I did.

Author's Note

I want to conclude this journey with two personal notes. In the early part of this book, I stated that my wife, Annie, had lost her smile. That needs to be amended now: Annie and I, along with our family, are smiling again and are grateful for having remained strong through a long and, at times, dark ordeal, as well as for having good friends and a great attorney who cared. This book has given me the chance to reflect on everything that occurred. Writing this book has allowed me to understand the true treasures in life better.

One final comment. You might have assumed I was guilty as you followed my story. After all, the federal government charged me with many serious crimes. You might have even thought about other parts of the story. Here's another white-collar criminal lining his pockets, getting rich at someone else's expense: his employer.

As I have stated, I knew I hadn't done anything wrong. I worked hard to help build a business that benefited my employer and colleagues. In my experience, most people found guilty of a crime claim they are innocent. Most are not. While some are innocent, I am one of those people who was. I could discuss the cost of this ordeal to me, both financially and mentally, but I choose not to. As previously stated, I am a lucky man. Added to my good fortune is the vindication received, thanks to my diligent lawyer, who fought for justice.

My greatest fortune is my family: my wife, children, and now our grandchildren. Consider my final comment and reflect on how our justice system operates. With all this in mind, perhaps the next time you read about someone accused of a crime, you can take a moment to wait for all the facts before jumping to conclusions. As they say, "You can't tell a book by its cover." Our media does its best to report 'the facts.' Don't we all love reading about someone caught with their hands in the cookie jar? Sometimes those facts aren't the whole story. Everyone deserves a fair hearing, and everyone has the right to be presumed innocent.

www.ingramcontent.com/pod-product-compliance
Lightning Source LLC
Chambersburg PA
CBHW052029030426
42337CB00027B/4923